Study Guide to Accompany
Managerial Economics, Third Edition

Study Guide to Accompany

Managerial Economics, *Third Edition*
by Ivan Png and Dale Lehman

Ivan Png and Joy Cheng

BLACKWELL PUBLISHING
350 Main Street, Malden, MA 02148-5020, USA
9600 Garsington Road, Oxford OX4 2DQ, UK
550 Swanston Street, Carlton, Victoria 3053, Australia

First published 2008 by Blackwell Publishing Ltd

1 2008

ISBN: 978-1-4051-8159-4

The Library of Congress has already cataloged the main work as follows:

Png, Ivan, 1957–
Managerial economics / Ivan Png and Dale Lehman.—3rd ed.
p. cm.
Includes bibliographical references and index.
ISBN 978-1-4051-6047-6 (pbk. : alk. paper) 1. Managerial economics.
I. Lehman, Dale E. II. Title.

HD30.22.P62 2007
338.5024′658—dc22 2006103321

Set in 10/12pt Times
by Graphicraft Limited, Hong Kong
Printed and bound in Singapore
by C.O.S. Printers Pte Ltd

For further information on
Blackwell Publishing, visit our website at
www.blackwellpublishing.com

Contents

Preface

This Study Guide supports *Managerial Economics*, *Third Edition*, by Ivan Png and Dale Lehman. Each chapter contains:

- Chapter summary
- Key concepts
- General objectives
- Notes
- Answers to Progress Checks
- Answers to selected Review Questions
- Worked answers to sample discussion questions

Please note that many questions have no definitive answer, and hence the answers provided here are only suggestive.

Kindly refer to the website at http://www.mecon.nus.edu.sg/ for updates, including errata.

Ivan Png
Joy Cheng

Chapter 1

Introduction to Managerial Economics

Chapter Summary

Managerial economics is the science of directing scarce resources to manage cost effectively. It consists of three branches: competitive markets, market power, and imperfect markets. A market consists of buyers and sellers that communicate with each other for voluntary exchange. Whether a market is local or global, the same managerial economics principles apply.

A seller with market power will have freedom to choose suppliers, set prices, and use advertising to influence demand. A market is imperfect when one party directly conveys a benefit or cost to others, or when one party has better information than others.

An organization must decide its vertical and horizontal boundaries. For effective management, it is important to distinguish marginal from average values, stocks from flows, and to consider the timings of actions. Managerial economics applies models that are necessarily less than completely realistic. Typically, a model focuses on one issue, holding other things equal.

Key Concepts

managerial economics
microeconomics
macroeconomics
economic model
marginal value
average value
stock
flow
other things equal
discounting
net present value
bounded rationality
market
vertical boundaries
horizontal boundaries
industry
market power
imperfect market
outsourcing

General Chapter Objectives

1. Define managerial economics and introduce students to the typical issues encountered in the field.
2. Discuss the scope and methodology of managerial economics. Distinguish a marginal concept from its average, and a stock concept from a flow. Describe the importance of the "other things equal" assumption in managerial economic analysis.
3. Introduce the importance of timing: static vis-à-vis dynamic model.
4. Discuss organizational boundaries.
5. Describe what constitutes a market, and discuss competitive markets and imperfect markets.
6. Emphasize the globalization of markets.

Detailed Notes

1. Managerial Economics.

(a) Definition. Managerial economics is the science of directing scarce resources to manage cost more effectively.

(b) Application. Managerial economics applies to:

i. Businesses (such as decisions in relation to customers, suppliers, competitors, or the internal workings of the organization), nonprofit organizations, and households.

ii. The "old economy" and "new economy" in essentially the same way except for two distinctive aspects of the "new economy": the importance of network effects and scale and scope economies.

(1) Network effects in demand – the benefit provided by a service depends on the total number of other users, e.g., when only one person had email, she had no one to communicate with, but with 100 million users on line, the demand for Internet services mushroomed;

(2) Scale and scope economies – scaleability is the degree to which scale and scope of a business can be increased without a corresponding increase in costs, e.g., the information in Google is eminently scaleable (the same information can serve 100 as well as 100 million users) and to serve a larger number of users, Google needs only increase the capacity of its computers and links.

iii. Both global and local markets.

2. Preliminaries.

(a) Scope.

i. Microeconomics – the study of individual economic behavior where resources are costly, e.g., how consumers respond to changes in prices and income, how businesses decide on employment and sales, voters' behavior, and setting of tax policy.

ii. Managerial economies – the application of microeconomics to managerial issues (a scope more limited than microeconomics).

iii. Macroeconomics – the study of aggregate economic variables directly (as opposed to the aggregation of individual consumers and businesses), e.g., issues relating to interest and exchange rates, inflation, unemployment, import and export policies.

(b) Methodology.

i. Fundamental premise – economic behavior is systematic and therefore can be studied. Systematic economic behavior means individuals share common motivations and behave systematically in making economic choices, i.e., a person who faces the same choices at two different times will behave in the same way both times.

ii. Economic model – a concise description of behavior and outcomes:

(1) Focuses on particular issues and key variables (e.g., price, salary), omits considerable information, hence unrealistic at times;

(2) Constructed by inductive reasoning;

(3) To be tested with empirical data and revised as appropriate.

(c) Margin vis-à-vis average variables in managerial economics analyses.

i. Marginal value of a variable – the change in the variable associated with a unit increase in a driver, e.g., amount earned by working one more hour;

ii. Average value of a variable – the total value of the variable divided by the total quantity of a driver, e.g., total pay divided by total no. of hours worked;

iii. Driver – the independent variable, e.g., no. of hours worked;

iv. The marginal value of a variable may be less that, equal to, or greater than the average value, depending on whether the marginal value is decreasing, constant or increasing with respect to the driver;

v. If the marginal value of a variable is greater than its average value, the average value increases, and vice versa.

(d) Stocks and flows.

i. Stock – the quantity of a given item at a specific point in time, measured in units of the item, e.g., items on a balance sheet (assets and liabilities), the world's oil reserves in the beginning of a year;

ii. Flow – the change in a given item over some period of time, measured in units per time period e.g., items on an income statement (receipts and expenses), the world's current production of oil.

(e) Holding other things equal – the assumption that all other relevant factors do not change, and is made so that changes due to the factor being studied may be examined independently of those other factors. Having analyzed the separate effects of each factor, we can then put them together for the complete picture.

3. Timing.

(a) Static/dynamic models

i. Static model describes behavior at a single point in time, disregarding differences in the sequence of actions and payments.

ii. Dynamic model explicitly focuses on the timing and sequence of actions and payments.

(b) Discounting is a procedure used to transform future dollars into an equivalent number of present dollars. It is necessary to discount future values so that they can be compared with the present.
(c) Net present value is the sum of the discounted values of a series of inflows and outflows over time.

4. Organization.

(a) Organizations include businesses, non-profits, and households.
(b) Organizational boundaries.
   i. Vertical boundaries – delineate activities closer to or further from the end user.
   ii. Horizontal boundaries are defined by the scale and scope of an organization's operations. Scale refers to the rate of production or delivery of a good or service and scope refers to the range of different items produced or delivered.
   iii. Organizations that are members of the same industry may choose different vertical and horizontal boundaries.
(c) Individual behavior.
   i. Rationality means that, when presented with various alternatives, individuals choose the alternative that gives them the greatest difference between value and cost.
   ii. Human beings behave with bounded rationality because they have limited cognitive abilities and cannot fully exercise self-control.

5. Markets.

(a) Markets.
   i. A market consists of buyers and sellers that communicate with one another for voluntary exchange. It is not limited by any physical structure.
   ii. In markets for consumer products, the buyers are households and sellers are businesses.
   iii. In markets for industrial products, both buyers and sellers are businesses.
   iv. In markets for human resources, buyers are businesses and sellers are households.
   v. An industry consists of the businesses engaged in the production or delivery of the same or similar items.
(b) Competitive markets.
   i. Markets with many buyers and many sellers, where buyers provide the demand and sellers provide the supply, e.g., the cotton market.
   ii. The demand-supply model – basic starting point of managerial economics, the model describes the systematic effect of changes in prices and other economic variables on buyers and sellers, and the interaction of these choices.

(c) Market power.
   i. Market power – the ability of a buyer or seller to influence market conditions. A seller with market power will have relatively more freedom to choose suppliers, set prices, and influence demand.
   ii. Businesses with market power, whether buyers or sellers, still need to understand and manage their costs.
   iii. In addition to managing costs, sellers with market power need to manage their demand through price, advertising, and policy toward competitors.

(d) Imperfect Market.
   i. In an imperfect market, one party directly conveys a benefit or cost to others, or where one party has better information than others.
   ii. The challenge is to resolve the imperfection and be cost-effective.
   iii. Imperfections can also arise within an organization, and hence, another issue in managerial economics is how to structure incentives and organizations.

6. Global integration.

(a) Local vis-à-vis global markets.
   i. Local markets – owing to relatively high costs of communication and trade, some markets are local, e.g., housing, groceries. The price in one local market is independent of prices in other local markets.
   ii. Global markets – owing to relatively low costs of communication and trade, some markets are global, e.g., commodities, shipping, financial services. For an item with a global market, the price in one place will move together with the prices elsewhere.
   iii. Whether a market is local or global, the same managerial economic principles apply.

(b) Communications costs and trade barriers. Falling costs of international transport and communication, and reduced trade barriers are causing markets to be more integrated across geographical border.

(c) Outsourcing. Outsourcing is the purchase of services or supplies from external sources (domestic or foreign). Foreign sources may provide cheaper skilled labor, specialized resources, or superior quality – resulting in lower production costs and/or improved quality.

Answers to Project Checks

1A. The managerial economics of the "new economy" emphasizes network effects in demand and scalability.

1B. NPV = 3 – 2/(1.02) = 2/(1.02)2 = –0.880, or –$880,000.

1C. Vertical boundaries delineate activities closer to or further from the end user. Horizontal boundaries are defined by the scale and scope of operations.

Answers to Review Questions

1. Marketing over the Internet is a scaleable activity. Delivery through UPS is somewhat scaleable: UPS already incurs the fixed cost of an international collection and distribution network; it may be willing to give Amazon bulk discounts for larger volumes of business.
2. No, models must be less than completely realistic to be useful.
3. (a) Average price per minute = (20 + 14.70 × 4)/5 = HK$15.76 per minute. (b) Price of marginal minute = HK$14.70.
4. Number of cars in service January 2007 + production + imports – exports – scrappage during 2007 = Number of cars in service January 2008. Number of cars in service is stock; other variables are flows.
5. False, in general. For a project where the costs come first and the benefits later, the statement is true.
6. The employer can invest an amount now which will accrue a return over time. What the employer requires is that the amount invested now together with the income over time equal $1 million at the time of paying the pensions.
7. [Omitted].
8. With strong economies of scale, the business should produce on a large scale, and hence its horizontal boundaries would be broader.
9. They are subject to bounded rationality owing to limited cognitive abilities and because they cannot fully exercise self-control.
10. (a) The electricity market includes buyers and sellers. (b) The electricity industry consists of sellers only.
11. (a) False. (b) False.
12. (a) Intel.
13. (b).
14. (a) and (b).
15. Competitive markets have large numbers of buyers and sellers, none of which can influence market conditions. By contrast, a buyer or seller with market power can influence market conditions. A market is imperfect if one party directly conveys benefits or costs to others, or if one party has better information than another.

Sample Answer to Discussion Question

1. Nancy's savings consist of $10,000 in a savings account that yields 2% a year interest and another $10,000 in a money market fund that pays interest of 5% a year. Nancy has just received a gift of $10,000 from his mother. Her bank pays 4% interest on savings accounts with a minimum deposit of $20,000. The money market fund pays 5% interest on investments up to $100,000.
   (a) Calculate the average interest rate (= dollar amount of interest divided by amount of investment) from the savings account if Nancy deposits the additional $10,000 in the savings account and qualifies for the higher interest rate.
   (b) Calculate the average interest rate if Nancy deposits the additional $10,000 in the money market fund.
   (c) Calculate the marginal interest rate (= increase in dollar amount of interest divided by additional investment) from the savings account if Nancy deposits the additional $10,000 in the savings account.
   (d) Calculate the marginal interest rate if Nancy deposits the additional $10,000 in the money market fund.
   (e) From the viewpoint of maximizing her total interest income, where should Nancy deposit the additional money?

Answer:

(a) Note that Nancy will receive the 4% rate on the entire $20,000 deposit. The average interest rate from the savings deposit = 4%.
(b) Average interest rate from money market fund = 5%.
(c) Marginal interest rate from the savings deposit = (800 – 200)/10,000 = 6%.
(d) Marginal interest rate from money market fund = 5%.
(e) Savings account: since it provides a higher marginal interest rate on the additional investment.

Part I

Competitive Markets

Chapter 2

Demand

Chapter Summary

A demand curve shows the quantity demanded as a function of price, other things equal. Generally, the demand curve slopes downward. Changes in price are represented by movements along the demand curve, while changes in other factors, such as income, the prices of related products, and advertising, are represented by shifts of the entire demand curve. The market demand curve is the horizontal summation of the individual demand curves of the various buyers.

For a normal (inferior) product, demand is positively (negatively) related to changes in buyer's income. Two products are complements (substitutes) if an increase in the price of one causes a fall (an increase) in the demand for the other.

Buyer surplus is the difference between a buyer's total benefit from some quantity of purchases and his or her actual expenditures. Changes in price affect buyer surplus through the price changes themselves as well as through changes in the quantity demanded.

Package deals consist of a fixed quantity of the item for a fixed payment. Two-part prices consist of a fixed payment and a charge based on usage. These are two ways by which sellers can extract surplus from buyers.

Key Concepts

individual demand curve
marginal benefit
normal product
inferior product
complement
substitute
market demand curve
horizontal summation
total benefit
buyer surplus
two-part price

General Chapter Objectives

1. Describe a demand curve and distinguish an individual and market demand curve.
2. Illustrate how the demand curve can be used to: (a) show the quantity demanded at a particular price, and (b) the price the buyer(s) are willing to pay for a particular quantity.

3. Understand the effect of changes in income on demand and distinguish inferior from normal products.
4. Understand the effect of changes in the prices of related products on demand and distinguish complements from substitutes.
5. Appreciate the use of GNP and GDP in estimating market demand and the role of income distribution in affecting the demand.
6. Describe buyer surplus and express it graphically. Describe the concepts of package deals and two-part prices, and show graphically how sellers can use these schemes to extract buyer surplus.
7. Understand the business demand for inputs and describe the factors influencing business demand.

Detailed Notes

1. **The demand curve.** A demand curve describes the quantity demanded of an item given its price, buyer's income, seller's advertising expenditure, and other relevant parameters.

2. **Individual demand.**
   (a) Construction.
      i. Definition: A graph showing the quantity (horizontal axis) (e.g., no. of movies watched per month) that the buyer will purchase at every possible price (vertical axis) (e.g., ticket price per movie).
   (b) Slope.
      i. Marginal benefit – the (psychic or monetary) benefit provided by an additional unit of the item.
      ii. The principle of diminishing marginal benefit – each additional unit of consumption or usage provides less benefit than the proceeding unit. Accordingly, the price that an individual is willing to pay will decrease with the quantity purchased.
      iii. Diminishing marginal benefit gives rise to a downward sloping marginal benefit curve (which is also the demand curve): the lower the price, the larger the quantity demanded.
   (c) Preferences.
      i. The procedure for constructing a demand curve relies completely on the consumer's individual preferences and this has two implications:
         (1) Demand curve will change with changes in the consumer's preferences, and
         (2) Different consumers may have different preferences and hence different demand curves.
   (d) Changes in income or other factors vis a vis a change in price on individual demand.

i. A change in the price of an item (holding income and all other factors unchanged) generally causes movement along an individual demand curve (a change in the quantity demanded).
ii. A change in income or other factors (e.g., the prices of related products, advertising, season, weather, and location) (other than the price of an item) causes an entire shift of the individual demand curve (a change in demand at all price levels).

3. Demand and income.

(a) Income changes.
  i. A change in income will affect individual demand at all price levels.
(b) Normal vis à vis inferior products.
  i. Normal products – demand is positively related to changes in buyer's income. Demand increases as buyer's income increases, and demand falls as buyer's income falls. When the economy is growing and income are rising, demand for normal products will rise and demand for inferior products will fall. The demand for normal products is relatively higher in richer countries.
  ii. Inferior products – demand is negatively related to changes in buyer's income. Demand increases as buyer's income decreases, and demand falls as buyer's income increases. In a recession where incomes are falling, demand for normal products will fall and demand for inferior products will rise. The demand for inferior products is relatively higher in poorer countries.
  iii. Broad categories (e.g., movies, transportation, consumer products) tend to be normal, while particular products within the categories (e.g., matinees, public transport, black and white TVs) may be inferior.
  iv. Distinction between normal and inferior products is important for business strategy and international business.

4. Other factors in individual demand.

(a) Complements and substitutes.
  i. Complements – two products are complements if an increase in the price of one causes a fall in the demand for the other; e.g., popcorn and movies.
  ii. Substitutes – an increase in the price of one causes an increase in the demand for the other; e.g., video rentals and movies.
  iii. In general, when there is an increase in the price of a complement or a fall in the price of a substitute, the demand curve shifts to the left.
(b) Advertising.
  i. Advertising may be informative as well as persuasive.
  ii. An increase in advertising expenditure generally increases individual demand.

iii. The effect of advertising expenditure on demand may be subject to diminishing marginal product – each additional dollar spent on advertising has a relatively smaller effect on demand.

(c) Durable goods. In the demand for consumer durables (e.g., automobiles, home appliances, and machinery), in addition to price, income, the prices of complements and substitutes, and advertising, three additional factors are relevant:

i. Expectations about future prices and incomes;

ii. Interest rates; and

iii. Prices of used models.

5. Market demand curve.

(a) Construction.

i. Definition: A graph showing the quantity that all buyers will purchase at every possible price. It is the horizontal summation of the individual demand curves.

ii. It enables businesses to understand the entire market rather than individual customers.

(b) Slope. All consumers get diminishing marginal benefit: the individual demand curve slopes downward, the market demand curve also slopes downward. At a lower price, the market as a whole will buy a larger quantity.

(c) The effect of changes in income or other factors vis a vis a change in price on market demand.

i. A change in the price of an item (holding income and all other factors unchanged) generally causes movement along the market demand curve from one point to another on the same curve.

ii. A change in income or other factors (e.g., the prices of related products, advertising) (other than the price of an item) causes a shift of the entire market demand curve.

iii. The directions of the effects of changes in income and other factors on market demand are similar to those for individual demand.

iv. Comparing market demands in different countries. Two ways of measuring the income of an entire country: the gross national product (GNP = GDP + income from foreign sources) and the gross domestic product (GDP = total value of production).

(d) Income distribution.

i. Common shortcut in estimating demand: by estimating the demand for an individual with average income (dividing the GNP or GDP by population) and multiply that by the number of buyers.

ii. However, the more uneven the distribution of income within a market, the more important it is to consider the actual distribution of income and not merely the average income.

6. Buyer surplus.

(a) As the individual demand curve shows the quantity that one buyer is willing and able to purchase at every possible price, a seller can calculate the maximum price that the buyer can be charged for a given purchase.

(b) Benefit.

  i. Marginal benefit: the benefit provided by an additional unit of an item, measured as the maximum amount that the buyer is willing to pay for that unit.

  ii. Total benefit: the benefit yielded by all the units that the buyer purchases, i.e., the marginal benefit from the first up to and including the last unit purchased. Graphically, this is the area under the buyer's demand curve up to an including the last unit purchased. This is the maximum that the buyer is willing to pay for that quantity, this is also the maximum price that a seller can charge.

(c) Benefit vis-à-vis price.

  i. Definition: The difference between an individual buyer's total benefit from some quantity of purchases and her or his actual expenditure.

  ii. Graphically reflected by the area between the demand curve and the price line.

(d) Price changes.

  i. Price reduction leads to increase in buyer's surplus: first, a lower price on the quantity that the buyer would have purchased at the original higher price; and second, as the buyer buys more (depending on the buyer's response to the price reduction), she gains buyer surplus on each of the additional purchases.

  ii. The buyer loses from a price increase: a higher price and a reduction in the quantity purchased.

(e) Package deals and two-part pricing. A seller can extract buyer surplus by the following:

  i. Package deal.

  ii. Two-part price – a pricing scheme consisting of a fixed payment and a charge based on usage (e.g., telephone monthly charge coupled with an airtime charge).

(f) Market buyer surplus – the sum of the individual buyer surpluses. Analysis similar to that of individual buyer surplus. Useful concept in analyzing impact of price changes on the market as a whole and in developing pricing policies to maximize a seller's profit.

7. Business demand.

(a) Inputs.

  i. Some items are purchased only by businesses (as inputs for the production of other goods and services for sale to consumers or other businesses), e.g., machine tools, human resources, TV commercials.

ii. Some items are purchased by both consumers (for final consumption or usage) and businesses, e.g., gasoline and telephone calls.
iii. The inputs purchased by a business can be classified into materials, energy, labor, and capital, which may be substitutes or complements.

(b) Demand.
i. The principles of business demand are similar to those underlying consumer demand.
ii. Principle of diminishing marginal benefit.
(1) A business can measure its marginal benefit from an input as the increase in revenue arising from an additional unit of the input, and will be subject to diminishing marginal benefit.
(2) The demand curve for an input by a business slopes downward due to the diminishing marginal benefit from the input.
(3) Business demand is derived from calculations of marginal benefit. A business should buy an input up to the quantity that its marginal benefit from the input exactly balances the price.

(c) Factors in demand.
i. A change in the price of an input is represented by a movement along the demand curve.
ii. Changes in other factors will lead to a shift of the entire demand curve.
(1) A major factor in consumer demand is income. Business demand does not depend on income but rather on the quantity of the output.
(2) The demand for an input also depends on the prices of complements and substitutes in the production of the output.
(3) On the whole, purchasing decisions of businesses are relatively less subject to impulse buying than those of consumers. Hence advertising plays a smaller role in business demand, and there is relatively more informative than persuasive advertising.

Answers to Progress Checks

2A. The theater must cut its price by $3 from $11 to $8.

2B. (1) It slopes downward because of diminishing marginal benefit.
(2) Assuming that all-in-one stereos are an inferior product, the drop in the consumer's income will cause the demand curve to shift to the right.

2C. Video rentals are a substitute for movies. A fall in the price of video rentals will cause the demand curve for movies to shift to the left.

2D. An increase in the price of a complement would cause the market demand to shift to the left.

2E. If the price of movies is $8, Joy's buyer surplus would be the area under her demand curve above the horizontal line at the price of $8.

Answers to Review Questions

1. [Omitted].
2. [Omitted].
3. Introduction of the new product will:
   (a) Reduce the demand for male condoms.
   (b) Reduce the demand for birth control pills.
4. Newspapers and free-to-the-air broadcast television are substitutes for cable television service. The controls limited competition for illegal cable television services and so boosted their demand.
5. Mobile and fixed-line telephone services are complements to the extent that subscribers of one service may call subscribers of the other. Mobile and fixed-line telephone services are substitutes to the extent that a user may subscribe to mobile service in place of fixed-line telephone service.
6. Pepsi advertising will increase the demand for the soft drink.
7. (a) The demand for Marriott rooms will increase. (b) Assuming that Motel 6 rooms are an inferior product, the demand for Motel 6 rooms will decrease.
8. Mont Blanc fountain pens are a luxury item and more sensitive to income distribution.
9. (a), (b), and (c).
10. The carrier should set the price so that the consumer has no buyer surplus.
11. [Omitted].
12. Not true. Each additional item provides less marginal benefit. Actual savings are the difference between total benefit and the price paid.
13. Consumer demand depends on income, while demand for inputs depends on the output quantity. Consumer demand is relatively more sensitive to advertising than business demand.
14. Banks install ATMs to substitute equipment for labor, and hence save on wages. It is relatively more profitable to make this substitution in countries where labor is expensive.
15. Ships are durable, and the demand for new ships depends on the prices of secondhand vessels and interest rates.

Sample Answer to Discussion Question

1. Using data from 93 countries, the Economist estimated a relationship between the literacy rate of female adults and the number of births per woman (fertility rate). When the literacy rate is 0%, the fertility rate is 8% per woman, and when the literacy rate is 100%, the birth rate is 2.5 per woman ("Population: Battle of the Bulge," Economist (September 3, 1994), pp. 19–21).
   (a) Construct a diagram with literacy rate on the vertical axis and fertility rate on the horizontal axis. Mark the two points that the Economist estimated. Join the two points with a straight line.
   (b) Perhaps the largest cost of having a baby is the time that the mother must invest to bear and rear the child. For a more educated woman, is the value of this time higher or lower?
   (c) Returning to your diagram, mark "cost of child" on the vertical axis. Does your diagram have any relation to a demand curve? Please explain.

Answer:

(a) The line will be downward sloping illustrating the inverse (negative) relationship between the two variables.
(b) Higher (the opportunity cost is higher).
(c) Yes. The higher the cost (price) the lower the quantity demanded (the quantity of children desired).

Chapter 3

Elasticity

Chapter Summary

The elasticity of demand measures the responsiveness of demand to changes in a factor that affects demand. Elasticities can be estimated for price, income, prices of related products, and advertising expenditures. The own-price elasticity is the ratio of the percentage change in quantity demanded to the percentage change in price, and is a negative number. Demand is price elastic if a 1% increase in price leads to more than a 1% drop in quantity demanded, and inelastic if it leads to less than a 1% drop in quantity demanded.

The own-price elasticity can be used to forecast the effects of price changes on quantity demanded and buyer expenditure. Elasticities can be used to forecast the effects on demand of simultaneous changes in multiple factors. All elasticities vary with adjustment time. The long-run demand is generally more elastic than the short-run demand in the case of nondurables, but not necessarily for durables.

Elasticities can be estimated from records of past experience or test markets using the statistical technique of multiple regression.

Key Concepts

elasticity of demand
own-price elasticity
arc approach
point approach
elastic
inelastic
income elasticity
cross-price elasticity
advertising elasticity
short run
long run
time series
cross section
dependent variable
independent variable
multiple regression

General Chapter Objectives

1. Describe the concept of elasticity.
2. Describe the arc approach and the point approach when deriving the own-price elasticity of demand and discuss the properties of own-price elasticity.

3. Discuss the intuitive determinants of price elasticity. Introduce the relationship between own-price elasticity and total revenue when there is a price change for an elastic and inelastic item.
4. Describe the application of income elasticity, cross-price elasticity, and advertising elasticity, as well as forecasting the effects of multiple factors on demand.
5. Explain the importance of time on elasticity.
6. Discuss the statistical estimation of elasticities.

Detailed Notes

1. Elasticity of demand.

(a) Definition: The responsiveness of demand to changes (increase or decrease) in an underlying factor (e.g., price of the product itself, income, prices of related products, advertising).
(b) Changes in any of these factors will lead to a movement along or shift of the demand curve.
(c) There is an elasticity corresponding to every factor (i.e., measuring the responsiveness of demand to changes in each factor) that affects demand.
(d) Elasticities depend on the time available for adjustment.
(e) With elasticities, managers can forecast the effect of single or multiple changes in the factors underlying demand.

2. Own-price elasticity.

(a) Every demand curve (including the individual demand curve and market demand curve) has a corresponding own-price elasticity.
   i. The own-price elasticity of demand is the percentage by which the quantity demanded will change if the price of the item rises by 1%.
   ii. Equivalently, it is the ratio: percentage (proportionate) change in the quantity demanded divided by the percentage (proportionate) change in price.
(b) Construction. There are 2 ways of deriving the own-price elasticity of demand.
   i. Arc approach: calculates the own-price elasticity of demand from the average values of observed price and quantity demanded.
   ii. Point approach: calculates own-price elasticity from a mathematical equation, in which the quantity demanded is a function of the price and other variables. The own-price elasticity is the coefficient of price.
   iii. For an infinitesimally small change in price, the arc estimate equals the point elasticity.
(c) Properties.
   i. It is a negative number (sometimes reported as an absolute number);
   ii. It is a ratio of two proportionate changes, and hence a pure number independent of units of measurement;

iii. It ranges from 0 (where a large % change in price causes no change in quantity demanded) to negative infinity (where an infinitesimal % change in price causes a large change in quantity demanded);

iv. Demand is considered price inelastic if a 1% increase in price leads to less than a 1% drop in the quantity demanded;

v. Demand is considered price elastic if a 1% increase in price leads to a greater than 1% drop in the quantity demanded.

(d) Intuitive factors affecting own-price elasticity.

i. Availability of direct or indirect substitutes affects the elasticity of demand. The fewer substitutes are available, the less elastic the demand. The more specifically defined the item (a particular brand of cigarettes), the more elastic will be its demand. The demand for the product category (cigarettes as a whole) will be relatively less elastic.

ii. Buyer's prior commitments.

iii. Benefits/costs of economizing. Cost relative to the benefit from searching for better prices.

(1) Buyers have limited time so they focus on items that account for relatively larger expenditures. 'Low involvement' products that those that get relatively little attention from buyers.

(2) The balance between the cost and the benefit of economizing also depends on a possible split between the person who incurs the cost of economizing and the person who benefits.

(e) Elasticity and slope.

i. Own-price elasticity describes the shape of only one portion of the demand curve.

ii. Whether the demand curve is a straight line or curved, the own-price elasticity can vary with changes in the price of the item.

iii. Even when the slope remains constant, the changes in price and quantity demanded along the demand curve mean the own-price elasticity will vary.

iv. The steeper is the demand curve, the less elastic is demand, and vice versa.

3. Forecasting quantity demanded and expenditure.

(a) Quantity demanded and expenditure.

i. Given the own-price elasticity of demand, a seller (both an individual seller or the entire market) can forecast the effect of price changes on quantity demanded (i.e., sales from the viewpoint of an individual seller) and buyer expenditure (quantity demanded x price) (i.e., revenue from the viewpoint of an individual seller).

ii. If demand is price inelastic, a seller can increase profit by raising price:

(1) A price increase causes the drop in quantity demanded (i.e., the drop in sales) to be proportionally smaller than the increase in price;

(2) Expenditure (and revenue) will increase; and

(3) As production is reduced, costs are lowered and profit increased.

iii. If demand is price elastic, and a seller raises the price:
   (1) The drop in quantity demanded will be proportionally greater than the increase in price; and
   (2) Expenditure will be reduced.

iv. Generally, it is in the best interest of a seller to raise the price until the demand becomes price elastic.

(b) Accuracy.
   i. Use of demand curve: more precise forecasts.
   ii. Use of own-price elasticity.
      (1) Not as precise as using the full demand curve as own-price elasticity may vary along a demand curve.
      (2) Does not provide as much information as the full demand curve.
      (3) Generally, the error in a forecast based on the own-price elasticity will be larger for larger changes in the price and the other factors that affect demand.
      (4) But managers seldom know the entire demand curve, as their information is limited to the quantity demanded around the current values of the factors that affect the demand.
      (5) Elasticities provide sufficient information for most business decisions.

4. Other elasticities.

(a) Income elasticity.
   i. Definition.
      (1) Percentage by which the quantity demanded will change if the buyer's income rises by 1%.
   ii. Construction.
      (1) Arc approach.
      (2) Point approach.
      (3) For an infinitesimally small change in income, the arc estimate equals the point elasticity
   iii. Properties.
      (1) With properties similar to those of own-price elasticity, but note a difference in that income elasticity can be a positive number.
      (2) It is a ratio of two proportionate changes, and hence a pure number independent of units of measurement.
      (3) Can range from negative infinity to positive infinity.
         a. Normal products (positive income elasticity): if income rises, demand rises.
         b. Inferior products (negative income elasticity): if income rises, demand falls.
      (4) Demand is considered income inelastic if a 1% increase in income leads to less than a 1% change in the quantity demanded.
      (5) Demand is considered income elastic if a 1% increase in income leads to a greater than 1% change in the quantity demanded.

iv. Factors affecting income elasticity.
   (1) Demand for necessities tends to be relatively less income elastic than the demand for discretionary items.
   (2) Changes in any of the other factors (including price) affecting demand.

(b) Cross-price elasticity.
   i. Definition.
      (1) Percentage by which the demand will change if the price of another item rises by 1%;
      (2) Other things equal (including the own price of the first item).
   ii. Properties.
      (1) Can range from negative infinity to positive infinity.
         a. Substitutes (positive cross-price elasticity): an increase in the price of one will increase the demand for the other. The more two items are substitutable, the higher their cross price elasticity.
         b. Complements (negative cross-price elasticity): an increase in the price of one will reduce the demand for the other.

(c) Advertising elasticity.
   i. Definition. Percentage by which the demand will change if the seller's advertising expense rises by 1%.
   ii. Most advertising is undertaken by individual sellers to promote their own business. By drawing buyers away from competitors, advertising has a much stronger effect on the sales of an individual seller than on the market demand. Advertising elasticity of the demand faced by an individual seller tends to be larger than the advertising elasticity of the market demand.

(d) Forecasting the effect of multiple factors. We can predict the percentage change in demand due to changes in multiple factors (sometimes pushing in different directions) by simply summing the percentage changes due to each separate factor, using the corresponding elasticities.

5. Factors affecting all elasticities: adjustment time.

(a) Buyers need time to adjust. Adjustment time is a factor that affects all elasticities (e.g., own-price elasticity).
   i. Distinguish between short run and long run.
   ii. Short run for the buyer – a time horizon within which a buyer cannot adjust at least one item of consumption or usage.
   iii. Long run for the buyer – a time horizon long enough for buyers to adjust all items of consumption or usage.

(b) Nondurables: the longer the time that buyers have to adjust, the bigger will be the response to a price change, and therefore the relatively more elastic the demand in the long run.

(c) Durables (e.g., automobiles): the difference between short- and long-run elasticities of demand depends on a balance between the time to adjust and the replacement frequency effect.

   i. Replacement frequency effect: For instance, with respect to income elasticity,
      (1) Short run – a drop in income will cause demand to fall more sharply in the short run.
      (2) Long run – the effects on sales will be muted.

(d) Forecasting demand. Just as short-run elasticities can be used to forecast the effect of multiple (short-run) changes in the factors that affect demand, we can also apply the same method to forecast the effect of long-run changes, using long-run elasticities in place of short-run elasticities.

6. Estimating elasticities. Elasticities can be estimated by the statistical technique of multiple regression.

(a) Businesses sell different products and or cater to different buyers, and face different demand curves and different elasticities.

(b) Data.
   i. Types of data.
      (1) Time series: a record of changes over time in one market, obtained by focusing on a particular group of buyers and observing how their demand changes as the factors affecting demand vary over time.
      (2) Cross section: a record of data at one time over several markets, obtained by comparing the quantities purchased in markets with different values of the factors affecting demand.
   ii. Compilation of data.
      (1) Past experience (e.g., statistics and records, public or private).
      (2) Surveys and experiments (e.g., test markets on genuine buyers making actual purchases).

(c) Specification.
   i. Dependent variable: the variable whose changes are to be explained.
   ii. Independent variable: a factor affecting the dependent variable.

(d) Multiple regression: a statistical technique to estimate the separate effect of each independent variable on the dependent variable.
   i. Aims to estimate values for constant and coefficients of independent variables.
   ii. The method of least squares seeks a set of estimated constant and coefficients to minimize the sum of the squares of the residuals (residual = difference between actual value of dependent variable and predicted value).

(e) Interpretation and statistical significance.
   i. Use the estimated constant and coefficients to calculate corresponding elasticities.
   ii. F-statistic and R-squared measure overall significance of the independent variables and the equation.
   iii. t-statistic measures significance of a particular independent variable.

Answers to Progress Checks

3A. The residential demand for water is relatively less elastic than the industrial demand.

3B. The demand curve is a straight line. At a price of \$110,000, the quantity demanded would be 14,000 while at a price of \$120,000, the quantity demanded would be 12,000. Accordingly, the proportionate change in the quantity demanded is $-2/13$ and the proportionate change in the price is $10,000/115,000 = 10/115$. Hence, by the arc approach, the own-price elasticity of demand is $(-2/13)/(10/115) = -1.77$.

3C. The demand for liquor is relatively more income elastic than the demand for cigarettes.

3D. For a durable, the short-run demand could be more or less elastic than the long-run demand.

3E. The advertising elasticity of demand is $0.03 \times 446.67/88.93 = 0.15$.

Answers to Review Questions

1. Many business travelers are traveling at the expense of others, so they spend less effort in economizing on price. Also, business travel is less discretionary and more of a necessity than leisure travel.

2. The person who decides on the service (doctor/patient) may be separate from the person who pays (medical insurer/health maintenance organization). Hence, the person who decides on the service spends little effort in economizing on price.

3. It is the percentage change in the quantity demanded divided by the percentage change in price. The percentage change in the quantity demanded is the change in quantity demanded divided by the average quantity demanded, and hence has no units. The percentage change in the price is the change in price divided by the average price, and hence has no units. The own-price elasticity is negative because a price increase leads to a decrease in the quantity demanded.

4. [Omitted].

5. Rise.

6. [Omitted].

7. (a) True; (b) True.

8. (b) Complements.

9. The elasticity with respect to changes in the price of Ferragamo shoes would be a smaller number.

10. The increase in quantity demanded would be $1.3 \times 5 = 6.5\%$.

11. Advertising by one product brand will draw customers from customers of other brands as well as increase the demand for beer in general. Advertising of beer in general can only increase the market demand.

12. More elastic in the long run.

13. For a nondurable item, demand takes time to adjust, hence the long-run demand is more elastic than the short-run demand. For a durable item, there is a countervailing effect: in response to changes in price or income, buyers adjust their replacement times and these adjustments cause larger changes in short-run demand than long-run demand.

14. By minimizing the sum of the squares of residuals, the method aims to minimize *both* instances of the predicted value exceeding the actual value of the dependent variable, and instances of the predicted value falling short of the actual value of the dependent variable. A method that minimized just the sum of the residuals would ignore instances of the predicted value falling short of the actual value of the dependent variable.

15. A cross section records all the data at one time, while a time series records changes over time.

Sample Answer to Discussion Question

2. At Boston-area service stations, the elasticity of the demand for gasoline with respect to price (combining the pure price effect with the effect on waiting times) was –3.3, the elasticity with respect to station fueling capacity was 0.7, and the elasticity with respect to the average price at nearby stations was 1.2 (Png & Reitman, 1984).

(a) Explain why the elasticity with respect to the average price at nearby stations is a positive number.

(b) Amy's station is the only competitor to Al's. Al's station has 3% more fueling capacity. Originally, both stations charged the same price. Then Amy reduced her price by 2%. What will be the percentage difference in quantity demanded between the two stations?

(c) If Amy raises capacity from 6 to 7 fueling places, by how much could she increase price without affecting sales?

Answer:

(a) Because they are substitutes – an increase in the price at nearby stations (e.g. by 1%) will raise the quantity demanded at the service station under consideration (e.g. by 1.2 %).

(b) Al's station has 3% greater fueling capacity. This implies that the quantity demanded at Al's station will be $3 \times 0.7 = 2.1\%$ greater. Amy's price is 2% lower, hence her quantity demanded will be $2 \times 1.2\% = 2.4\%$ greater. The combined effect implies that Al's station will have 0.3% less quantity demanded than Amy's station.

(c) Amy's fueling capacity increases by 1/6 or 16.67%. This would raise her quantity demanded by $16.67 \times 0.7 = 11.669\%$. Suppose that she can raise price by $X\%$ without affecting sales. This would reduce quantity demanded by $X \times 3.3 = 3.3X\%$. Hence, we need $11.669 = 3.3X$, which implies that $X = 3.5$.

Chapter 4

Supply

Chapter Summary

A small seller, which cannot affect the market price, maximizes profit by producing at a rate where its marginal cost equals the price. (For a small seller, the price equals marginal revenue.) In the short run, at least one input is fixed and therefore cannot be adjusted. The business breaks even when total revenue covers variable cost. In the long run, the business can adjust all inputs and leave or enter the industry. It breaks even when total revenue covers total cost.

The supply curve shows the quantity supplied as a function of price, other things equal. The effect of a change in price is represented by a movement along the supply curve to a new quantity. Changes in other factors such as wages and the prices of other inputs are represented by shifts of the entire supply curve.

Seller surplus is the difference between revenue from some production rate and the minimum amount necessary to induce the seller to produce that quantity. Elasticities of supply measure the responsiveness of supply to changes in underlying factors that affect supply.

Key Concepts

short run
long run
fixed cost
variable cost
total cost
marginal cost
average (unit) cost
marginal product
marginal revenue
profit maximizing
total revenue
sunk cost
individual supply curve
market supply curve
seller surplus
elasticity of supply
price elasticity of supply

General Chapter Objectives

1. Explain why short run costs vary with the production rate.
2. Introduce the concept of diminishing marginal product.

3. Determine the profit-maximizing production rate in the short run and explain the break-even condition in the short run. Explain why the demand for inputs is derived from the production rate.
4. Appreciate that, in the long run, supply can change with the entry of new businesses and exit of existing businesses. Determine the profit-maximizing production rate in the long run and explain the breakeven condition in the long run.
5. Describe how the market supply curve is derived in the short run and the long run and their properties.
6. Describe seller surplus in words and determine it graphically.
7. Describe the elasticity of supply concept, calculate price elasticity of supply coefficients and interpret them.

Detailed Notes

1. **Individual supply**: short run and long run.

(a) Whether to continue in production and how much to produce depends on costs and revenues.

(b) Time horizon.

   i. Short run – time horizon in which a seller cannot adjust one or more inputs. In the short run, the business must work within the constraints of past commitments such as employment contracts and investment in facilities and equipment.

   ii. Long run – time horizon long enough for a seller to adjust all inputs and production.

2. Short run costs.

(a) Fixed vis à vis variable costs.

   i. Based on estimates of expenses on rent, wages, and other supplies needed at various production rates (scales of operation).

   ii. Fixed cost = cost of inputs that do not change with the production rate. The entire fixed cost is a sunk cost, i.e., a cost that has been committed and cannot be avoided.

   iii. Variable cost = cost of inputs that change with the production rate.

   iv. Total cost = sum of fixed cost and variable cost (C = F + V).

(b) Marginal cost = the change in total cost (i.e., variable cost) due to the production of an additional unit.

(c) Average cost.

   i. Average fixed cost = fixed cost divided by the production rate.

   ii. Average variable cost = variable cost divided by the production rate.

   iii. Average (total) cost (also called unit cost) = the sum of average variable cost and average fixed cost; also equals total cost divided by the production rate.

   iv. Marginal product.

(1) Definition. The increase in output arising from an additional unit of the input.
(2) Diminishing marginal product from the variable inputs: the marginal product becomes smaller with each increase in the quantity of the variable input.

v. Average total cost (average cost) generally first drops with increase in the production rate and then rises.
(1) When the production rate is higher, the fixed costs will be spread over more units, the average fixed cost will be declining.
(2) When the production rate is higher:
a. At first, the average variable cost falls (as the variable inputs match the fixed input relatively better);
b. Then, the average variable cost rises (as more of the variable inputs are added in combination with the fixed input, there will be a mismatch, leading to a diminishing marginal product from the variable inputs).

(d) Technology. At every production level, the total, average, and marginal cost depend on the seller's individual operating technology.
i. The curves will change with adjustments in the seller's technology. E.g., a seller that discovers a technology involving a lower fixed cost will lower its average cost curve; a seller that uses a technology with a lower variable cost will lower its average, average variable, and marginal cost curves; and
ii. Different sellers may have different technologies and, hence, different cost curves. They may differ in the structure of fixed vis-à-vis variable costs. Some may have better technologies and hence lower costs than others

3. Short run individual supply.

(a) Assumptions.
i. Business aims to maximize profit.
ii. The business is so small relative to the market that it can sell as much as it would like at the going market price.

(b) Production rate.
i. The total revenue of a business is the price of its product multiplied by the number of units sold.
ii. Marginal revenue = the change in total revenue arising from selling an additional unit.
iii. If continuing in production, profit = total revenue – total cost; Profit = R – F – V.
iv. The profit-maximizing scale of production is where marginal revenue equals marginal cost (where the total revenue line and the total cost curve climb at exactly the same rate).
(1) Whenever the marginal revenue exceeds the marginal cost, profit will be raised by increasing production.

(2) Whenever the marginal revenue is less than the marginal cost, profit will be raised by reducing production.

v. When a business can sell as much as it would like at the market price, marginal revenue equals price (it does not have to reduce price to sell more units); and therefore, the profit-maximizing rule for such a business becomes that production rate at which price equals marginal cost.

(c) Break even. To decide whether to continue production at all.

i. If the business shuts down, it must pay the fixed cost, though not the variable cost; profit = –F.

ii. A business should continue in production:

(1) If the maximum profit from continuing in production is at least as large as the profit from shutting down; i.e., if the business breaks even.

(2) Short run break even condition: so long as total revenue covers variable cost; or equivalently, so long as average revenue (price) covers average variable cost.

(3) Sunk costs should be ignored in making a current decision. A sunk cost is a cost that has been committed and cannot be avoided.

(d) Individual supply curve.

i. A graph showing the quantity that one seller will supply at every possible price. It shows the minimum price that the seller will accept for each unit of production.

ii. It is identical to that part of the marginal cost curve above the minimum point of the average variable cost curve.

iii. For every possible price of its output, a business should produce at the rate that balances its marginal cost with the price, provided that the price covers average variable cost.

iv. As marginal cost rises when production is expanded, a seller should expand production only if it receives a higher price.

v. A change in the price of the output generally causes movement along a supply curve.

(e) Input demand.

i. As the costs of inputs change, the marginal cost curve shifts up or down, the profit-maximizing scale of production changes, the demand for inputs also changes.

ii. By varying the cost of a particular input, we can determine the quantity demanded of that input at every possible cost and construct the seller's demand for that input.

iii. As the quantity demanded of the input will be higher at a lower input price, the demand curve will slope downward.

4. Long run individual supply.

(a) Long run costs.

i. Based on estimates of expenses on rent, wages, and other supplies needed at various production rates when all inputs are avoidable.

ii. The business may incur some costs even at a production level of zero, e.g., maintenance of minimum size facility.
iii. Long run average cost curve is lower and has a gentler slope than that of the short run. In the long run, the seller has more flexibility in adjusting inputs to changes in the production rate, and can thus produce at a lower cost. In the short run, it may not be able to change one or more inputs.

(b) Production rate. The profit-maximizing rule is to produce where price equals long run marginal cost (essentially the same in the long run as for the short run).

(c) Break even. To decide whether to continue production at all.
i. If the business shuts down, it will incur no costs (as all costs are avoidable in the long run); profit = 0.
ii. A business should continue in production:
(1) If the maximum profit from continuing in production is at least as large as the profit from shutting down; i.e., if the business breaks even.
(2) Long run break even condition: so long as its total revenue covers total cost; or equivalently, so long as average revenue (price) covers average total cost.

(d) Individual supply curve: long run.
i. The long run individual supply curve is identical to that part of the long run marginal cost curve above the minimum point of the long run average total cost.

5. **Market supply.** The market supply curve is the horizontal summation of the various individual sellers' supply curves. The market supply curve begins with the seller that has the lowest average variable cost, then blends in sellers with higher average variable cost.

(a) Short run.
i. The market supply curve.
(1) It is a graph showing the quantity that the market will supply at every possible price of the output.
(2) The effect of a change in the price of an output is represented by a movement along the supply curve.
(3) A change in the price of an input will affect an individual seller's marginal cost at all production levels and shift the entire marginal cost curve. Such changes will also shift the market supply curve.
ii. Properties. The market supply curve generally slopes upward. If the price of the output is higher, each individual seller will wish to produce more, and the market as a whole will also produce more.

(b) Market supply: long run.
i. The market supply curve.
(1) It is a graph showing the quantity that the market will supply at every possible price of the output.
(2) The effect of a change in the price of an output is represented by a movement along the supply curve.

(3) A change in the price of an input and other factors than the price of output will cause a shift in the entire market supply curve.

ii. Properties.

(1) For any change in price, the long-run market supply slopes more gently (i.e., is more elastic) than the short-run market supply.

a. The freedom of entry and exit is a key difference between the short run and the long run: In the long run, every business has complete flexibility in deciding on inputs and production.

b. Sellers whose total revenue cannot cover total costs will leave the industry until all remaining sellers break even.

c. An industry where businesses are profitable (i.e., total revenue exceeds total costs) will attract new entrants. This will increase market supply and reduce market price (pushing down the profit of all sellers):

i. If the existing sellers continue making profits, new entrants will enter the industry;

ii. Some sellers may leave or enter the market until all sellers just break even.

(2) The long-run market supply curve may be completely flat. In the long run, the quantity supplied can expand through replication of existing businesses.

a. However, the long-run market supply curve may slope upward. The resources available to various suppliers may vary in quality. New entrants may not be able to replicate the resources (especially in resource-based industries and where location is important) of existing suppliers and will incur higher costs.

6. Seller surplus.

(a) A seller's profit varies with the price of its output.

(b) Price vis-à-vis marginal cost. Seller's surplus = difference between a seller's revenue from some production rate and the minimum amount necessary to induce the seller to produce that quantity.

i. In the short run, it is equal to the difference between total revenue from some production rate and the variable cost, or R – V.

ii. In the long run, it is equal to the difference between total revenue from some production rate and the total cost.

(c) Purchasing. A buyer can extract the seller's surplus. The buyer should design a bulk order and pay the seller the minimum amount to induce production at the desired level, i.e., the buyer should purchase up the seller's marginal cost curve.

(d) Market seller surplus.

i. Market seller surplus = difference between the market revenue from some production rate and the minimum amount necessary to induce the market to produce that quantity.

(1) It is equal to the sum of the individual seller surpluses; and
(2) It is represented graphically by the area between the price line and the market supply curve (in both the short run and the long run).

ii. In the long run:
(1) If the market supply curve is flat, there will be no market seller surplus;
(2) If the market supply curve slopes upward, there will be some market seller surplus. Seller surplus accrues to those who own the superior resources.

7. Elasticity of supply.

(a) Elasticity of supply.
i. Measures the responsiveness of supply to changes in an underlying factor (such as the price of the item and inputs). There is an elasticity corresponding to every factor that affects supply.

(b) Price elasticity of supply. It is the percentage by which the quantity supplied will change if the price of the item rises by 1%, other things equal.
i. Calculated by using the arc approach or point approach and interpreting the resulting number.

(c) Properties.
i. A pure number that does not depend on any units of measure.
(1) Generally the supply curves of businesses selling goods and services slope upward, so the price elasticity of supply is a positive number ranging from 0 to infinity.
(2) If the price elasticity is less than 1, supply is inelastic.
(3) If the price elasticity is more than 1, supply is elastic.
ii. It may vary along the same supply curve.
iii. A change in any of the factors that affect supply may affect the price elasticity.

(d) Intuitive factors.
i. Capacity utilization affects both individual and market supply elasticities, e.g., if capacity is tight, the seller may not increase production much even if the price rises substantially, and supply will be relatively inelastic.
ii. Time under consideration. In the short run, some inputs may be costly or impossible to change, the marginal cost of production will be steep and supply inelastic. In the long run, the marginal cost of production will slope more gently, and an individual and market supply curve will be more elastic.

(e) Forecasting quantity supplied. A change in price will affect revenue:
i. Directly; and
ii. Through changing the sales or quantity supplied (using the price elasticity).

Answers to Progress Checks

4A. The total cost curve would be higher but the variable cost curve would not change.

4B. The marginal and average variable cost curves would not change, but the average cost curve would be lower.

4C. To maximize profit, Luna must produce at the rate where marginal cost equals 75 cents. Please refer to figure 4C on page 443 of the textbook.

4D. If the market price of eggs is \$1.31, Luna should produce 8,000 dozen eggs a week and its revenue would be \$1.31 × 8,000 = \$10,840, hence its profit would be \$10,480 – \$7,232 = \$3,248.

4E. See figure 4E on page 443 of the textbook.

4F. Proportionate change in quantity = (6,500 – 5,800)/6,150 = 11%. Proportionate change in price = (90 – 80)/85 = 12%. Hence, the price elasticity = 11/12 = 0.9.

Answers to Review Questions

1. The short run is a time horizon within which a seller cannot adjust at least one input. By contrast, the long run is a time horizon long enough that the seller can adjust all inputs. Assuming that all fixed costs are also sunk, while all variable cost are not sunk, then there are fixed costs only in the short run, while all costs are variable in the long run.
2. This statement confuses average with marginal cost. The average cost is \$2. The marginal cost may be greater than, equal to, or less than \$2, depending on the production technology.
3. Nothing. Marginal costs are not necessarily related to fixed costs.
4. The marginal revenue is the change in total revenue arising from the sale of an additional unit. If the business can sell as much as it wants at the market price, then the additional unit can be sold at the market price without affecting the price at which the original units are sold. Hence, the marginal revenue equals the price.
5. Since the price is less than the marginal cost, the producer can raise profit by reducing production.
6. The analysis underestimates the increase in profit: It considers only the increase in profit on the existing production, and ignores the increase in profit resulting from an increase in production.
7. (a) Increases both average and marginal cost curves. (b) No effect. (c) Reduces both average and marginal cost curves.
8. Like any other input, advertising is subject to diminishing marginal product. Each additional dollar of advertising yields a smaller increment in sales and profit.
9. Not necessarily. In the short run, a business that is covering its variable cost should continue in production.
10. The bus operator that suspended operations may have realized that the price fell below its average variable cost, while the other that continued in business may have had an average variable cost that was below the price.
11. (a) Movement along the market supply curve. (b) Shift of the entire market supply curve. (c) Shift of the entire market supply curve.
12. The buyer should design its order to leave the seller with zero seller surplus.
13. (a) False. (b) True.
14. If the supply curve is more elastic, the increase in seller surplus will be larger. (Note: This assumes same increase in price of the product.)
15. The supply will be relatively more elastic in the long run.

Sample Answer to Discussion Question

5. Dynamic random access memory (DRAM) chips are an essential component of personal computers, mobile telephones, and other electronic devices. Over the course of the 1990s, DRAM technology evolved through several generations – from 4 Megabits to the present state-of-the-art 4 Gigabit chips. Until 1998, there were two major American manufacturers of DRAMs – Texas Instruments (TI) and Micron Technology. Then, TI sold its factories in Avezzano (Italy), Richardson (Texas), and Singapore, and interests in two Asian joint ventures to Micron Technology. TI shut the remainder of its DRAM production facilities including one in Midland, Texas.

(a) Which probably had the higher average cost – the Richardson or Midland plant?

(b) Compare the effects on the world wide long-run DRAM supply of TI's sale of the Richardson plant with its closure of the Midland factory.

(c) Explain Micron's decision to buy TI's plants in terms of differences between the two companies in their expectations of long-run DRAM prices.

Answer:

(a) The Midland plant probably had the higher average cost, which explains why TI could not sell it and had to shut it.

(b) TI's sale of the Richardson factory did not change the worldwide long-run supply of DRAMs. Its closure of the Midland factory did reduce the supply.

(c) Micron's forecast of long-run DRAM prices may have been higher than TI's.

Chapter 5

Competitive Markets

Chapter Summary

How will an increase in demand and a reduction in marginal costs affect the market for an item? Questions such as these are commonplace. The answers, however, are not so simple. To understand the complete effect of a shift in demand or supply, it is necessary to consider both sides of the market. Generally, the effect of any change in demand or supply depends on the elasticities with respect to price of both demand and supply.

The time horizon is a key factor affecting the elasticities of demand and supply. Prices are more volatile and quantity adjustment takes relatively longer in industries where production involves substantial sunk costs.

Key Concepts

perfect competition
market equilibrium
excess supply
excess demand
short-run market equilibrium
long-run market equilibrium

General Chapter Objectives

1. Introduce why the demand-supply framework is the core of managerial economics.
2. Describe the characteristics of perfect competition.
3. Determine market equilibrium, explain why it exists and how it may change.
4. Explain the impact of a change in supply on market price and quantity, and explain the dynamics involved in moving from an initial equilibrium to a new market equilibrium.
5. Explain the impact of a change in demand on market price and quantity, and explain the dynamics involved in moving from an initial equilibrium to a new market equilibrium.
6. Compare the impact of a change in demand or supply on the short- vis-à-vis long-run market equilibrium.

Detailed Notes

1. **Introduction.** It is important to consider both demand and supply when predicting the impact of any change on price and quantity. Even though only one side of the market may be changing initially, it is necessary to consider the interaction with the other side to obtain a complete picture.

2. **Perfect competition.**
   (a) The demand-supply framework (perfect competition) is the core of managerial economics. It can be applied to address business issues in a wide range of markets, including goods and services, consumer as well as industrial products, and items sold in domestic and international markets.
   (b) Market demand and supply.
      i. When deriving a market demand curve, it is assumed that every buyer can purchase as much as she would like at the going price and all buyers pay the same price.
      ii. When deriving a market supply curve, it is assumed that every seller can deliver as much as she would like at the going price and all sellers receive the same price.
   (c) For a market to be in equilibrium, neither buyers nor sellers may face rationing.
   (d) Five conditions for perfect competition. If a market meets the five conditions for perfect competition, we can validly apply the concepts of demand and supply. A market is said to be in perfect competition if:
      i. Its products are homogeneous (i.e., they are perfect substitutes).
         (1) Competition in a market where products are differentiated (e.g., mineral water, owing to chemical and marketing differences) is not as keen as that in a market where products are homogeneous.
         (2) Generally, prices for differentiated products are different.
      ii. It includes many small buyers, each purchasing a quantity that is small relative to the market.
         (1) In a market where some buyers have market power, different buyers pay different prices: The buyers with market power get lower prices.
         (2) Where some buyers have market power, it is not possible to construct the market demand curve as the buyers with market power can affect the going price.
      iii. It includes many small sellers, each supplying a quantity that is small relative to the market.
         (1) Where some sellers have market power, it is not possible to construct market supply curve as the sellers with market power can affect the going price.

iv. There is free entry and exit, i.e., new buyers and sellers can enter freely, and existing buyers and sellers can exit freely. There are no technological, regulatory or legal barriers.
   (1) With free entry and exit, the market price cannot stay above a seller's average cost for very long.
   (2) If the market price is above a seller's average cost, new sellers will enter, add to the market supply, and bring down the price.

v. All buyers and all sellers have symmetric information about market conditions, e.g., prices, substitutes, and technology.
   (1) Markets where there are differences in information among buyers, among sellers, or between buyers and sellers, are not as competitive as those where all buyers and sellers have equal information.

3. Market equilibrium.

(a) Demand and supply. Market equilibrium is the price at which the quantity demanded equals the quantity supplied (a price in which there is neither a surplus nor a shortage).
   i. The price will not tend to change: the quantity demanded just balances the quantity supplied.
   ii. Purchases will not tend to change: buyers maximize benefits less expenditure.
   iii. Sales will not tend to change: sellers maximize profits.

(b) Excess supply: the amount by which the quantity supplied exceeds the quantity demanded.
   i. If the market price is above equilibrium, buyers will cut back purchases.
   ii. Sellers will compete to clear their extra capacity, and market price would drop back toward the equilibrium level.
   iii. The higher the price above equilibrium, the larger will be the excess supply.

(c) Excess demand (a shortage): the amount by which the quantity demanded exceeds the quantity supplied.
   i. If the market price is below equilibrium, buyers will compete for the limited available quantity.
   ii. The market price would tend to rise to the equilibrium level.
   iii. The lower is the price below equilibrium, the larger will be the excess demand.

(d) Significance of equilibrium.
   i. If a market is not in equilibrium, buyers or sellers will push the market toward equilibrium. Applying the concept of market equilibrium and comparing market equilibria, we can predict the impact on price and quantity given changes in demand or supply (where there is a change in an economic variable, e.g., the price of a related product, the cost of inputs, or government policy).

ii. Very few markets exactly satisfy all five conditions for perfect competition. We can still apply the demand – supply analysis but must check the implications against the unsatisfied conditions.

4. Supply shift.

(a) Changes in economic variables (e.g., changes in the cost of inputs, or government policy) that shift the entire supply curve would:
  i. Increase supply at every price: a downward (rightward) shift in the supply curve of the output; or
  ii. Decrease supply at every price: upward (leftward) shift in the supply curve of the output.

(b) Equilibrium change. To understand the impact of a supply shift, we need to consider the interaction between supply and demand.

(c) The change in the equilibrium price depends on the price elasticities of both demand and supply.
  i. When *demand* is extremely elastic, buyers are extremely sensitive to price. When the supply curve shifts, buyers soak up all the additional quantity supplied, and the equilibrium price remains unchanged.
  ii. When *supply* is extremely inelastic, sellers are completely insensitive to price (they provide the same quantity regardless of the price of the output or costs of inputs). When the cost of inputs changes, sellers provide the same quantity, and the equilibrium price remains unchanged.
  iii. When *demand* is extremely inelastic, buyers are completely insensitive to price (they purchase the same quantity regardless of the price). When the supply curve shifts, buyers purchase the same quantity, and the equilibrium price changes by the same amount as the supply shift.
  iv. When *supply* is extremely elastic, the marginal cost of production is constant. If an input cost changes, the marginal cost changes by the same amount at all production levels. When the supply curve shifts, the equilibrium price changes by the same amount as the supply shift.
  v. If demand is more elastic than supply, then the change in the equilibrium price resulting from a shift in supply will be smaller.
  vi. If demand is less elastic than supply, then the change in the equilibrium price resulting from a shift in supply will be larger.
  vii. A downward or upward shift in the supply curve will change the equilibrium price (to the new equilibrium price) by no more than the amount of the supply shift.

(d) Common misconception. There is a common misconception is that if seller's costs fall by some amount, then the market price will fall by the same amount. Realistically,
  i. Demand is somewhat elastic and sensitive to price.
  ii. Supply is somewhat elastic and sensitive to price.

5. Demand shift.

(a) Changes in economic variables (e.g., changes in prices of complements or substitutes, or government policy) that shift the entire demand curve would:
   i. Increase demand at every price: an upward (rightward) shift in the demand curve of the output; or
   ii. Decrease demand at every price: downward (leftward) shift in the demand curve of the output.

(b) Equilibrium Change. To understand the impact of a demand shift, we need to consider the interaction between supply and demand.

(c) The change in the equilibrium price depends on the price elasticities of both demand and supply.

(d) There is a common misconception is that if demand increases by some amount, then the market quantity will increase by the same amount. This overlooks:
   i. The impact of a demand shift on sellers: the marginal cost of producing an additional unit of output might change.
   ii. The price sensitivity of buyers: the amount buyers are willing to pay for an additional unit of output.

6. Adjustment time.

(a) As the elasticities of demand and supply vary with the time horizon under consideration, shifts in demand and supply may have different short-run and long-run effects.

(b) When a market is in both short-run and long-run equilibrium:
   i. For each individual buyer, the quantity purchased: where marginal benefit equals price.
   ii. For each individual seller, the quantity provided: where marginal cost equals price.
   iii. At the equilibrium price, the market demand curve (horizontal summation of individual demand curves) crosses the market supply curve (horizontal summation of individual supply curves).
   iv. The equilibrium price signals to each buyer and seller the amount to purchase and provide, respectively.

(c) Short-run equilibrium.
   i. Definition: the price at which the short-run quantity demanded equals the short-run quantity supplied.
   ii. For each individual seller: short-run marginal cost equals market price.

(d) Long-run equilibrium.
   i. Definition: the price at which the long-run quantity demanded equals the long-run quantity supplied.
   ii. For each individual seller: long-run marginal cost equals market price.

(e) Demand increase. Starting from short and long-run equilibria. Assuming that short and long-run demand curves are the same.

- i. New short-run equilibrium.
  - (1) Higher price.
  - (2) Every seller expands its operations.
    - a. If the short-run marginal cost curve is steep, the price increase will not lead to a large expansion of operations; and vice versa.
    - b. The steepness of the short-run marginal cost curve depends on factors like availability of excess production capacity and overtime costs.
- ii. New long-run equilibrium.
  - (1) Higher price.
  - (2) Every seller expands its operations and new sellers enter the market.
    - a. The market supply curve tends to be more elastic in the long run (all costs become avoidable, freedom of entry and exit) than in the short run.
    - b. The industry will expand along the long-run supply curve.
    - c. Every seller breaks even: No more new entry or exit.

(f) Demand reduction.

- i. New short-run equilibrium.
  - (1) Lower price.
  - (2) Every seller cuts back its operations.
    - a. Sellers whose average variable cost exceeds the price will shut down.
    - b. Sellers whose average variable cost is covered by the price will remain in business.
    - c. Extent of cut back in operations depends on two factors:
      - i. In the short run (as opposed to the long run), some costs are sunk (prior commitments by sellers). A seller will continue to produce so long as its average variable cost is covered by the price.
      - ii. Slope of the seller's short-run marginal cost curve. If the slope is steep, a price reduction will not cut back operations by very much.
- ii. New long-run equilibrium.
  - (1) Lower price.
  - (2) Smaller number of sellers.
    - a. The market supply curve tends to be more elastic in the long run (all costs become avoidable, freedom of entry and exit) than in the short run. Note: Sellers whose long-run price is below their average total cost will exit the industry.
    - b. Entire industry contacts along the long-run market supply curve.
    - c. Every seller breaks even: with average total cost equal to the market price.
- iii. Market supply is more elastic in the long-run than in the short-run:
  - (1) The price in the long-run equilibrium is higher than in the new short-run equilibrium but lower than in the original equilibrium, and

(2) The quantity in the new long-run equilibrium is less than in the new short-run equilibrium, which in turn is less than in the original equilibrium.

(g) Price and quantity over time.

i. In response to shifts in demand, the market price will be more volatile in the short run than the long run.

ii. In response to shifts in demand, adjustment of production will be concentrated in the long run. There is a greater change in the market quantity over the long run than in the short run.

iii. The disparity between the short run and long run is relatively sharper in industries where operations involve substantial sunk costs. In such industries, the price will be relatively volatile, as the market adjusts to shifts in demand. When demand increases, owing to the substantial sunk costs, relatively little adjustment in production can be made in the short run.

iv. Long run demand may be more or less elastic than short run demand.

Answers to Progress Checks

5A. A seller with market power could affect the selling price; hence, it could not answer the question, "How much would you sell, assuming that you could sell as much as you would like at the going price?" Thus, it is not possible to construct a market supply curve.

5B. See figure 5B on page 444 of the textbook.

5C. (1) False. (2) True.

5D. See figure 5D on page 444 of the textbook.

5E. See figure 5E on page 445 of the textbook.

Answers to Review Questions

1. (b).

2. Refer to pp. 118–120 of the textbook.

3. True, because a seller with market power cannot sell as much as it would like at any particular price.

4. These regulations raise barriers to entry, and hence reduce the degree of competition.

5. False.

6. (a) New zero-calorie sweetener would shift the demand for sugar to the left. (b) Cut in farm wages would shift the supply of sugar to the right.

7. The quantity supplied will exceed the quantity demanded.

8. Excess demand.

9. (a) Reduce the supply. (b) Increase the demand (unless it causes a shift from apartment rentals to home ownership, in which case demand could decrease).

10. If the demand is extremely elastic or the supply is extremely elastic.

11. The wage increase would reduce the supply. Generally, the effect of any change in supply depends on the price elasticities of both demand and supply.

12. In the short run, price will increase by more and quantity will increase by less than in the long run.

13. The supply of new housing is more elastic in the long run than the short run. Hence, the price will rise further in the short run than the long run, while the quantity will increase more in the long run than the short run.
14. False. If sunk costs are substantial, sellers will quit production only if the price drops by a large amount. Hence, prices will be more volatile.
15. Sunk costs are relatively larger in supply by pipeline than tanker. Hence, prices would be more volatile in the market supplied by pipeline.

Sample Answer to Discussion Question

1. At times, a major problem for Japanese consumer electronics manufacturers has been the appreciation of the yen against the U.S. dollar. This means that the yen is more expensive in terms of the U.S. dollar.
   (a) Explain how the appreciation of the yen from ¥150 to ¥100 per U.S. dollar affects the wholesale cost of supplying Japanese consumer electronics to the United States.
   (b) Suppose that the Japanese yen rises by one-third against the U.S. dollar. Which of the following are plausible explanations of why the U.S. retail price of Japanese-made CD players will rise by less than one-third: (i) The wholesale cost accounts for only part of retailers' costs; (ii) American retail demand for Japanese-made CD players is inelastic; (iii) American retail supply of Japanese-made CD players is inelastic?
   (c) How will the appreciation of the yen affect the price and sales of Korean CD players in the United States?

   Answer:

   (a) An appreciation of the yen (depreciation of the dollar) will increase the price of Japanese consumer electronics to Americans – in this case by 50% (the dollar price of the yen increased from 100 to 150, or 50%).
   (b) (i) and (iii), because if the supply is more inelastic, then the change in the equilibrium price resulting from a shift in supply will be smaller.
   (c) The demand for Korean CD players will increase in the United States because Korean CD players are a substitute for Japanese CD players. As a consequence of the increase in the demand for Korean CD players, their prices and sales will rise.

Chapter 6

Economic Efficiency

Chapter Summary

The central idea in this chapter is Adam Smith's invisible hand. Free-market competition will ensure that the allocation of resources is economically efficient. Although the buyers and sellers act selfishly, the net outcome is at least as good as the best efforts of the most enlightened and well-informed central planner.

The same general principle applies within an organization. Through decentralization, management can achieve efficient use of scarce resources. This means charging a transfer price for items produced and consumed within the organization.

It is important to distinguish a payment or receipt from incidence. A payment or receipt can be shifted from one to the other side of the market. Incidence is fundamental and depends only on the elasticities of demand and supply. As an example, the incidence of taxes generally does not depend on whether the tax is collected from the buyers or the sellers in a market. It will be shared, according to the relatively elasticities of demand and supply, in either case.

Key Concepts

economic efficiency
technical efficiency
invisible hand
market or price system
outsourcing
cost and freight price
ex-works price
incidence
transfer price
tax incidence

General Chapter Objectives

1. Introduce the concept of economic efficiency.
2. Define three sufficient conditions for economic efficiency.
3. Discuss how Adam Smith's invisible hand, i.e., the market price, achieves economic efficiency in a perfectly competitive market.
4. Apply the three conditions for economic efficiency to a single organization and discuss the efficiency of de-centralization.

5. Apply the concept of incidence, distinguish it from payment, and understand how it depends on the elasticities of demand and supply.

Detailed Notes

1. Concept of economic efficiency.

(a) A guide to managing resources within an organization and across entire economies.
(b) Identifies opportunities for profit (there is a way to make money by resolving an economic inefficiency).
(c) A way to assess intermediation.

2. Conditions for economic efficiency.

(a) An allocation of resources (quantity) is economically efficient where no reallocation of resources can make one person (human being or business) better off without making another person worse off.
(b) Three sufficient conditions for economic efficiency:
  i. All users achieve same marginal benefit;
  ii. All suppliers operate at same marginal cost; and
  iii. Every user's marginal benefit = every supplier's marginal cost. When marginal benefit is less than marginal cost, society overall could gain by reducing provision of that item, and vice versa.
(c) Philosophical basis.
  i. Economic efficiency distinguished from technical efficiency.
    (1) Technical efficiency is the provision of an item at the minimum possible cost; it does not imply scarce resources are being well used.
    (2) Economic efficiency extends beyond technical efficiency. The quantity of an item supplied must be such that the marginal benefit equals the marginal cost.
  ii. It assesses resource allocations in terms of each individual user's evaluation of the benefit.
(d) Internal organization.
  i. Bank (businesses: commercial and individual banking) example:
    (1) Users: lending units.
    (2) Suppliers: deposit-taking units.
  ii. Three conditions.
    (1) Same marginal benefit. If one lending unit gets more profit than another, the company should switch some funds to the more profitable lending unit. The company's overall profit will be higher.
    (2) Same marginal cost. If one deposit-taking unit can produce funds at a lower marginal cost than another, then the company should direct the lower cost deposit-taking unit to produce more and the higher

cost deposit-taking unit to produce less. The company's overall profit will be higher.

(3) Marginal benefit = marginal cost. If the marginal benefit of funds to the lending units is less than the marginal cost of production, the company should cut back deposit-taking. The reduction in benefit would be less than the reduction of cost. The company's overall profit will be higher.

3. Adam Smith's "Invisible Hand".

(a) Perfect competition achieves economic efficiency. The invisible hand that guides multiple buyers and sellers, acting independently and selfishly, to channel scarce resources into economically efficient uses, is the market price.

(b) Competitive market. The market price communicates necessary information and provides concrete incentives:
   i. Users buy until marginal benefit equals price (to maximize benefit);
   ii. Producers supply until marginal cost equals price (to maximize profit);
   iii. Users and producers face same price.

(c) Market system. The market or price system is the economic system in which resources are allocated through the independent decisions of buyers and sellers, guided by freely moving prices.

4. De-centralized management.

(a) Internal market. A transfer price is the price charged for the sale of an item within an organization.

(b) Implementation. Decentralized management: Achieving economic efficiency within an organization.
   i. If there is a competitive market for an item, the transfer price should be set equal to the market price.
   ii. Right of outsourcing: consuming units within an organization should be allowed to outsource (i.e., outsourcing is the purchase of services or supplies from external sources).
   iii. Producing unit should be able to sell the product to outside buyers.
   iv. The 3 conditions for economic efficiency are satisfied. The internal market will be integrated with the external market.

(c) Example of commercial and individual banking:
   i. Users: lending units. Every lending unit maximizes profit and is permitted to buy funds at the market price (up to the point where marginal benefit balances market price) from any supplier, whether internal deposit-taking units or an outside source. Since all lending units face the same market price, their marginal benefits will be equal.
   ii. Suppliers: deposit-taking units. Managers of every deposit-taking unit maximize profit and sell funds at the market price (up to the point where marginal

cost balances the market price) to either internal lending units or outside buyers. Since all deposit-taking units face the same market price, their marginal costs will be equal.

iii. Since the lending units and the deposit-taking units face the same market price, marginal benefit equals marginal cost.

5. Incidence.

(a) Freight inclusive pricing vis-à-vis ex-works price:
   i. The "cost and freight (CF) price" includes the cost of delivery to the buyer.
   ii. The "ex-works price" does not include the cost of delivery to the buyer.

(b) Graphical representation:
   i. Represent CF price (paid by seller) by shifting the supply curve up by the cost of freight.
   ii. Represent ex-works price (paid by buyer) by shifting the demand curve down by the cost of freight.
   iii. Note: final equilibrium price and quantity the same with CF or ex-works pricing.

(c) Incidence. Incidence is the change in the price for a buyer or seller resulting from a shift in demand or supply. The incidence of freight charges and rokerage fees depends not on who pays the charge/fee, only on the price elasticities of demand and supply.

(d) Taxes. Some taxes are levied on consumers, others on businesses, and some are levied on both. As a result of the tax, there will be a new equilibrium. The price is higher and the quantity is smaller.

(e) Buyer's vis-à-vis seller's price. The seller's price is the buyer's price minus the amount of the tax.

(f) Tax incidence.
   i. Aside from administrative and psychological differences, the effect of a tax will be the same, whether it is collected from the buyers or the sellers. Further, the tax is generally shared between buyers and sellers according to their relatively price elasticities. The side of the market that is relatively less sensitive to price changes will bear the relatively larger portion of the tax.
   ii. With moderate demand and supply elasticities, the buyer's price will rise by less than the amount of the tax, the seller's price will drop by less than the amount of the tax, and the quantity will fall by some amount.

Answers to Progress Checks

6A. Technical efficiency means producing wheat at the minimum possible cost, while economic efficiency requires providing the quantities such that all users have the same marginal benefit, all producers operate at the same marginal cost, and the marginal benefit equals the marginal cost.

6B. The invisible hand increased the price of grain, which encouraged consumers to conserve and producers to grow more.

6C. With decentralization, Jupiter should set the transfer price equal to the market price of semiconductors. Then, both divisions will use semiconductors up to the point where marginal benefit equals the transfer price. This will ensure economic efficiency.

6D. See figure 6D on page 446 of the textbook.

6E. See figure 6E on page 447 of the textbook. The buyer's price increases relatively more. Hence, the incidence of the tax on travelers will be relatively higher.

Answers to Review Questions

1. Children were using bread (in sport) up to the point that the marginal benefit equaled the very low price. This price was less than the marginal cost. Hence, the marginal benefit of use was less than the marginal cost and not economically efficient.

2. The condition that all users receive the same marginal benefit.

3. In a competitive labor market, all buyers (employers) purchase up to the quantity where the marginal benefit equals the wage, and all sellers (workers) supply up to the quantity where the marginal cost equals the wage. Buyers and sellers face the same wage; hence, the allocation of labor is economically efficient.

4. If no resources are scarce (a highly improbable situation), then there is no need to allocate them. Central planning would be as effective as a market system.

5. [Omitted].

6. The juice division should be charged the market price of apples.

7. If the regulated business belongs to a perfectly competitive industry, then it would set the transfer price for any service equal to the market price. Hence, the government regulation does not impose any burden.

8. The retailers receive the wholesale price cut. In a competitive retail market, however, the wholesaleprice cut will increase the supply. The new equilibrium will have a lower retail price. Consumers benefit from a lower retail price, so part of the wholesale price cut will be incident on consumers.

9. Airlines and passengers.

10. Retail supply will decrease and demand will increase. The new equilibrium price (with free shipping) should be higher than without free shipping.

11. Payment refers to who conveys the money to the government. Incidence refers to the impact in terms of price – buyer's price and seller's price.

12. Since demand is inelastic and supply is very elastic, the tax will be incident mostly on the demand side. Manufacturers would not be much affected.

13. Demand is elastic relative to supply, so most of the sales tax in Philadelphia will be paid by the electronics store.

14. If the demand for these luxury items is inelastic, then the tax would not change consumption of these items by much.

15. The tax credit was essentially a subsidy. This can be represented by either by shifting up the demand curve or shifting down the supply curve. The credit would have been shared between manufacturers/ retailers of solar energy systems and consumers.

Sample Answer to Discussion Question

1. The Japanese consume relatively more fish and less meat than people in other developed countries. In 1995, then Worldwatch Institute President Lester R. Brown pronounced: "[I]f the Chinese were to consume seafood at the same rate as the Japanese do, China would need the annual world fish catch" (Who Will Feed China? New York, NY: W.W. Norton, 1995, page 30).

(a) Compare the Japanese marginal benefit from eating fish with that of other people. Which aspect of the philosophical basis of economic efficiency did Mr Brown overlook?

(b) How would increases in the Chinese demand for fish affect the world price of fish and Japanese fish consumption?

(c) Is it likely that China would consume the entire world fish catch?

Answer:

(a) The Japanese may have a stronger preference for fish than other peoples, hence their marginal benefit is higher. The concept of economic efficiency evaluates resource allocations according to each person's individual preferences.

(b) Increases in the Chinese demand for fish would raise the world price of fish and reduce Japanese fish consumption.

(c) No. The price of fish would rise to the point that the Chinese would eat substitutes.

Part II

Market Power

Chapter 7

Costs

Chapter Summary

Conventional accounting statements do not always provide all the information on costs necessary for effective business decisions. Managers should use the principles presented in this chapter to develop accurate information about costs.

Economies of scale arise from either significant fixed costs or variable costs that diminish with the scale of production. An industry where businesses exhibit scale economies will tend to be concentrated. Economies of scope arise from significant joint costs across the production of two or more items. Scope economies drive businesses to supply multiple products. The experience curve shows how average costs decline with cumulative production.

Opportunity cost is the net revenue from the best alternative course of action. Sunk costs are costs that have been committed and cannot be avoided. For effective business decisions, managers should consider opportunity costs and ignore sunk costs. The transfer price of an item within an organization should be set equal to the marginal cost.

Key Concepts

economies of scale
diseconomies of scale
economies of scope
diseconomies of scope
joint cost
experience curve
relevance
opportunity cost
economic value added
transfer price

General Chapter Objectives

1. Appreciate that conventional accounting statements do not always present the information needed for effective managerial decisions. Discuss the concept of scale economies, relate it to fixed costs, and apply it to business strategy.
2. Introduce the concept of diseconomies of scale.

3. Discuss the concept of scope economies, relate it to joint costs, and apply it to business strategy. Introduce the concept of diseconomies of scope.
4. Distinguish the experience curve from economies of scale.
5. Appreciate and apply the concept of opportunity cost, and specifically, to the capital of an organization.
6. Explain the objective and application of transfer pricing.
7. Appreciate and apply the concept of sunk cost.
8. Apply the statistical technique of multiple regression to cost analysis.

Detailed Notes

1. Economies of scale.

(a) Costs depend on the scale (production rate) and scope (variety of different products) of the business.
  i. Fixed cost: cost of inputs that do not change with scale.
  ii. Variable cost: cost of inputs that change with scale.
  iii. Note: some costs are partly fixed and partly variable.
  iv. Marginal cost: change in total cost due to the production of an additional unit; equals the rate of change of the variable cost.
  v. Average cost: total cost divided by scale; equals to the sum of average fixed cost and average variable cost.

(b) Definition – "Economies of scale" means that the average cost decreases with the scale of production.
  i. "Economies of scale" and "increasing returns to scale" are synonymous.
  ii. Marginal cost will be lower than the average cost.
  iii. Any increase in production will reduce the average cost.
  iv. Average cost curve slopes downward.

(c) Intuitive factors.
  i. Substantial fixed inputs.
    (1) At a larger scale, the cost of fixed inputs will be spread over more units, so that the average fixed cost will be lower.
    (2) If the average variable cost is constant or does not increase much with scale, the average cost will fall with scale.
  ii. Average variable costs that fall with scale, e.g., pipeline. Note: whether the average variable cost increases or falls with scale depends on the particular technology of the business.

(d) Strategic implications.
  i. Large scale operations (lower average cost).
  ii. Mass marketing, relatively low pricing.
  iii. Concentrated industry – few suppliers. Extreme case: monopoly.

2. Diseconomies of scale.

(a) Definition: Diseconomies of scale means that the average cost increases with the scale of production.
   i. "Diseconomies of scale" and "decreasing returns to scale" are synonymous.
   ii. Average cost curve is U-shaped (e.g., in the case of a perfectly competitive industry).

(b) Intuitive factors.
   i. Nonsubstantial fixed cost and variable cost rise more than proportionately with scale.
      (1) Initially, the cost of fixed inputs will be spread over more units, so the average fixed cost will be lower.
      (2) The average variable cost rises more than proportionately with scale.
      (3) There is a scale where the decreasing average fixed cost is outweighed by the increasing average variable cost.
      (4) The average cost reaches a minimum and rises with further increases in scale.

(c) Strategic implications.
   i. Small scale.
   ii. Niche marketing, relatively high pricing.
   iii. Fragmented industries. Extreme case: perfect competition.

3. Economies of scope and diseconomies of scope.

(a) Economies of scope.
   i. Definition: Economies of scope means that the total cost of production is lower with joint than with separate production.
   ii. Intuitive factors.
      (1) Significant joint costs. Joint cost: the cost of inputs that do not change with the scope of production.
   iii. Strategic implications.
      (1) Multiproduct suppliers dominate industries with economies of scope.
      (2) Though brand extension, the owner of an established brand can introduce new products at relatively lower cost than a competitor with no established brand.
   iv. Core competence: generalized expertise in the design, production, and marketing of products based on common or closely related technologies.

(b) Diseconomies of scope.
   i. Definition: Diseconomies of scope means that the total cost of production is higher with joint than with separate production.
   ii. Intuitive factors.
      (1) Insignificant joint costs.
      (2) Making one product increases the cost of making the other in the same facility.

iii. Strategic implications.
   (1) Produce products separately. Specialized production.

4. Experience Curve. The experience curve is distinct from economies of scale.

(a) The experience curve (also called the learning curve) shows how the unit (average) cost of production falls with cumulative production over time.
(b) Intuitive factors. Accumulated experience matters in industries characterized by relatively short production runs and a relatively substantial input of human resources, e.g., aerospace manufacturing and shipbuilding.
(c) The experience curve relates cumulative production over preceding periods to production costs in one period. Economies of scale relate the scale of production within one period to production costs in the same period.
(d) Strategic implications. Accurate forecasting of cumulative production would be crucial for both planning investments and setting prices.

5. Opportunity cost.

(a) Principle of relevance: managers should consider only relevant costs and ignore all others.
(b) Uncovering relevant costs. An analysis of the alternative courses of action for the decision at hand will uncover relevant costs. Two ways to uncover relevant costs:
   i. Explicit approach: consider the revenues and costs of alternative courses of action.
   ii. Opportunity cost approach: consider the net revenue from the best alternative course of action (i.e., the opportunity cost).
(c) Opportunity cost of capital.
   i. Economic value added is the net operating profit after tax subject to adjustments for accounting conventions less a charge for the cost of capital. This is a better measurement of business performance than accounting earnings.
   ii. Managers who evaluate business performance in terms of economic value added are less likely to be biased in favor of capital intensive activities and financing investment through equity.

6. Transfer pricing.

(a) To maximize the profit of the entire organization, the transfer price of an internally produced input should be set equal to its marginal cost.
(b) Perfectly competitive market for the input.
   i. Set transfer price equal to the market price (also equals marginal cost).

(c) Full capacity. Production of the input is subject to full capacity.
   i. Marginal cost curve is vertical and marginal cost is not well defined.
   ii. Set transfer price equal to the opportunity cost of the input, which is the marginal benefit that input provides to the current user.

7. Sunk cost.

(a) Alternative courses of action. An analysis of the alternative courses of action will identify sunk costs in a conventional accounting statement. Sunk cost: a cost that has been committed and cannot be avoided once incurred.
(b) Avoidable costs.
   i. The division of costs into sunk and avoidable depends on past commitments and planning horizon.
      (1) The longer the planning horizon, the more time there will be for past commitments to unwind and greater the freedom of action.
      (2) In the long run, all inputs are freely adjustable, so there will be no sunk costs.
   ii. The division of avoidable costs into fixed and variable elements depends on the technology of the business.
(c) Strategic implications.
   i. Should ignore sunk costs. Should consider only avoidable costs.
   ii. Managers should be careful about committing costs that will become sunk.
   iii. Two ways of dealing with sunk costs:
      (1) Explicitly consider the alternative courses of action.
      (2) Remove all sunk costs from the income statement.
(d) Sunk vis-à-vis fixed costs.
   i. Fixed cost: cost of inputs that do not change with the production rate. Give rise to economies of scale in the long run.
   ii. Some fixed costs become sunk once incurred, e.g., design cost for the first set of shoe molds.
   iii. Not all sunk costs are fixed, e.g., the second set of shoe molds as production increases.
   iv. Not all fixed costs become sunk when incurred.

8. Statistical methods: multiple regression.

(a) To analyze statistical data on costs and research the relationship between costs and the scale and scope of production.
(b) Example: the use of multiple regression analysis to investigate the extent of fixed costs and economies of scale in the production of elevator systems.
   i. Dependent variable: total cost; independent variables: factors that affect production costs (e.g., capacity, speed, travel, and number of landings).

ii. If the intercept term is positive and statistically significant, then there is a fixed cost.

(c) Forecasting. The estimated coefficients from a multiple regression can be used to forecast the dependent variable at various combinations of the independent variables.

(d) Other Applications. Multiple regression can also be applied to investigate the presence of joint costs across two products.

Answers to Project Checks

7A. See figure 7A on page 448 of the textbook.

7B. Neither economies nor diseconomies of scope.

7C. See figure 7C on page 448 of the textbook.

7D. The revenue from a shutdown in table 7.5 would become \$460,000 and the opportunity cost in table 7.6 would become \$680,000. Eleanor should continue in the warehouse business.

7E. In table 7.7, the columns for "Cancel Launch" would have zero in every cell. In table 7.8, the advertising agency cost would be \$50,000, and the Road Runner would charge \$250,000. Sol should cancel the launch.

7F. The cost would be $-5.51 + (21.20 \times 0.75) + (19.63 \times 1.5) + (0.04 \times 40) + (2.19 \times 10) =$ 63.335 thousand dollars, or \$63,335.

Answers to Review Questions

1. Economies of scale mean that average cost declines with the scale of production. Economies of scope mean that total cost declines with the scope of production.

2. Southern Power's average fixed cost will rise.

3. Economies of scale are more significant in (a).

4. No.

5. Economies of scope.

6. Diseconomies of scope.

7. Economies of scale mean that average cost declines with the scale of production at any given time. The experience curve means that average cost declines with the accumulated production over time.

8. Two reasons: first, the client's time must be spent getting a sales pitch, and second, the cost to the salesman will be reflected in the final price paid by the client.

9. If business performance is measured in terms of accounting profit, management may make decisions that reduce actual profit. For instance, they might ignore opportunity costs of capital. Economic value added is a better measure of performance.

10. The "profit" should be reduced by the opportunity cost of the facilities.

11. The transfer price of lumber should be the market price.

12. No. They are sunk costs.

13. (a).

14. (a).

15. Capacity, speed, and landings – the statistically significant variables.

Sample Answer to Discussion Question

1. Qantas operates a fleet of over 100 Boeing jet aircraft. Many jets carry cargo in their "bellies", under the passenger seating areas. Consider each of the following costs. Identify which are joint costs of passenger and belly cargo services, which are fixed costs of passenger service, and which are both.
   (a) Cockpit personnel: All jets, large and small, require a pilot and co-pilot. Belly cargo service requires no additional officers in the cockpit.
   (b) Airport landing fees: Some airports charge landing fees by weight of the aircraft, while others levy a fixed fee, regardless of weight.
   (c) Fuel: Larger aircraft and those carrying heavier loads will consume relatively more fuel.

   Answer:

   (a) Joint cost, and also a fixed cost.
   (b) If the landing fee varies with weight, then it is not joint or fixed. If a jet carries an additional 100 pounds of cargo, the airline must pay additional fees. Similarly, if the jet carries an additional passenger. If the landing fee is fixed, then it is a joint cost and a fixed cost.
   (c) Neither a joint cost, nor a fixed cost. If a jet carries an additional 100 pounds of cargo, the airline must spend more on fuel. Similarly, if the jet carries an additional passenger.

Chapter 8

Monopoly

Chapter Summary

Market power arises from unique resources, intellectual property, scale and scope economies, product differentiation, or regulation.

A seller with market power restrains sales to raise the market price above the competitive level and extract higher profits. It maximizes profit by operating at a scale where marginal revenue equals marginal cost. The extent to which a monopoly should adjust the price in response to changes in demand or costs depends on the shapes of both the marginal revenue and the marginal cost curves.

The profit-maximizing advertising-sales ratio is the incremental margin percentage multiplied by the advertising elasticity of demand. The profit-maximizing R&D-sales ratio is the incremental margin percentage multiplied by the R&D elasticity of demand.

A buyer with market power restrains purchases to depress the price below the competitive level and raise its net benefit.

Key Concepts

monopoly
monopsony
inframarginal units
contribution margin
promotion
incremental margin
incremental margin percentage
advertising-sales ratio
R&D-sales ratio
perfectly contestable market
Lerner Index
marginal expenditure

General Chapter Objectives

1. Introduce the concept of market power.
2. Enumerate and explain the different sources of market power.
3. Analyze how a seller with market power determines its profit-maximizing output and price level.

4. Explain how a seller with market power should adjust price and output in response to changes in demand and cost.
5. Analyze how much a seller with market power should spend on advertising, and adjust advertising in response to changes in price and cost.
6. Analyze how much a seller with market power should spend on R&D.
7. Compare and contrast output and price under monopoly and perfect competition.
8. Analyze how a monopsony determines its net benefit maximizing purchase and price.

Detailed Notes

1. Introduction.

(a) A seller (buyer) with market power can influence market demand (supply), price, and quantity demanded (supplied).
(b) Monopoly: the only seller in the market.
(c) Monopsony: the only buyer in the market.

2. Sources of market power.

(a) Sources of market power for monopolies (and monopsonies) are barriers that deter or prevent entry by competing sellers (buyers).
  i. Unique resources, e.g., unique human, physical or natural resources.
  ii. Intellectual property, e.g., ownership of patents or copyrights over inventions or expressions.
  iii. Economies of scale and scope, e.g., electricity distribution; cable TV and local telephone service.
  iv. Product differentiation through advertising, promotion, product design and distribution.
  v. Regulation, e.g., the government may award exclusive franchises (intended to avoid duplication and reduce cost of the service) for distribution of electricity, natural gas, and local telephone service.
(b) Additional source of market power for a monopsony: the existence of a monopoly. A seller that has a monopoly over some good or service is likely to have market power over the inputs into that item, e.g., national governments monopolize defense. By this monopoly, the government would have market power over suppliers of military equipment and supplies, as well as the services of military personnel.

3. Monopoly Pricing.

(a) A monopoly:
  i. Faces a downward sloping market demand curve.
  ii. Can either set price and let the market determine how much to buy, or set the quantity supplied and let the market determine the price, but not both.

(b) Revenue. Consider a monopoly that sets the price and lets the market determine the quantity of sales.
   i. Assumption: Profit maximization.
   ii. Profit = total revenue (price × sales) less cost.
   iii. Marginal revenue is the change in total revenue arising from selling an additional unit. It is the price of the marginal unit minus the loss of revenue on the inframarginal units. Inframarginal units are those other than the marginal unit.
   iv. Marginal revenue could be negative.
   v. To sell additional units, the price must be reduced.
   vi. Price generally exceeds marginal revenue, and the difference depends on the elasticity of demand.
      (1) If demand is very elastic, the seller need not reduce the price very much to increase sales, the marginal revenue will be close to price.
      (2) If demand is very inelastic, the seller must reduce the price substantially to increase sales, the marginal revenue will be much lower than price.

(c) Costs. Total cost generally increases with the scale of production. Marginal cost is the change in total cost due to the production of an additional unit. The change in total cost arises from change in the variable cost.

(d) Profit-maximizing price.
   i. Contribution margin is the total revenue less variable cost.
   ii. Change in contribution margin for an additional unit sold = marginal revenue – marginal cost
   iii. Profit-maximizing scale of operation is where:
      (1) Marginal revenue equals marginal cost, or
      (2) The sale of an additional unit results in no change to the contribution margin.

(e) Economically inefficient choice of production. Where marginal benefit exceeds marginal cost, a profit can be made through resolving the inefficiency.

4. Demand and cost changes.

(a) Changes in demand. A monopoly's response to changes in demand depends on both the new demand (new marginal revenue) and the original marginal cost.

(b) Marginal cost change. A monopoly's response to changes in cost depends on both the original demand (original marginal revenue) and the new marginal cost.

(c) The new profit maximizing price and scale depend on the shapes of both the marginal revenue and marginal cost curves. The monopoly should adjust its price until the marginal revenue equals marginal cost.

(d) Fixed cost change. Changes in fixed cost do not affect marginal cost, and will not affect the profit maximizing price and scale; unless, however, that fixed cost is so large that total cost exceeds total revenue, then the monopoly will shut down.

5. Advertising.

(a) A monopoly has market power and can influence demand (changes in demand and/or elasticity of demand). Promotion is the set of marketing activities that a business undertakes to communicate with its customers and sell its products.

(b) Benefit of advertising. The net benefit of advertising is the change in contribution margin less advertising expenditure.

(c) Advertising-sales ratio. The profit-maximizing advertising-sales ratio is the incremental margin multiplied by the elasticity of demand.
   i. The incremental margin is the price less the marginal cost or the increase in the contribution margin from selling an additional unit, holding the price constant.
   ii. The incremental margin percentage is the ratio of the price less the marginal cost to the price.
   iii. The elasticity of demand with respect to an increase in advertising is the percentage by which demand will change if the seller's advertising expenditure rises by 1%, other things equal.

(d) A seller should spend more on advertising:
   i. if the incremental margin percentage is higher, as each dollar of advertising produces relatively more benefit as measured by the incremental margin percentage. This means that, whenever a seller raises its price or its marginal cost falls, it should also increase advertising expenditure;
   ii. if either the advertising elasticity of demand or the sales volume is higher, as the influence of advertising on buyer demand is relatively greater.

6. Research and Development.

(a) Profit-maximizing level of R&D expenditure. The profit-maximizing R&D-sales ratio (the ratio of the R&D expenditure to sales volume) is the incremental margin percentage multiplied by the R&D elasticity of demand.

(b) A seller should increase R&D expenditure relative to sales volume:
   i. when the incremental margin percentage is higher (higher price or lower marginal cost);
   ii. if either the R&D elasticity of demand or the sales volume is higher.

(c) Project evaluation.
   i. Decisions on individual R&D projects should account for the timing of costs and benefits.
   ii. Most R&D projects are multi-stage. There may be an opportunity to abandon or modify a project as more information about costs, technical feasibility, and market demand becomes available.
   iii. The real options approach to investment decisions. R&D is viewed as analogous to a European call option, where the purchaser has the right, but not the obligation, to exercise the option at a future date.

7. Market Structure.

(a) Perfect competition (a market with numerous sellers, each too small to affect market conditions) vis-à-vis monopoly.
   i. Market price: The monopoly restricts production below the competitive level and can set a relatively higher price. Competition (and under specific conditions, even potential competition) pushes the market price down toward the long run average cost and results in more production.
   ii. The profit of a monopoly exceeds what would be the combined profit of all the sellers if the same market were competitive.

(b) Potential competition.
   i. A monopoly in a perfectly contestable market (one where sellers can enter and exit at no cost) cannot raise its price substantially above its long run average cost. Other sellers can profit by entering the market. The resulting increase in supply will drive the market price back toward the long run average cost.
   ii. The degree to which a market is contestable depends on the extents of barriers to enter and exit (e.g., liquidation costs).

(c) Lerner Index.
   i. The Lerner Index is the incremental margin percentage (ratio of the price less marginal cost to the price).
   ii. It measures the degree of actual and potential competition in a market.
   iii. It enables comparison of monopoly power in markets with different prices.
      (1) Perfectly competitive market: price equals marginal cost, hence the incremental margin = 0.
      (2) With potential competition: if a monopoly sets a price close to its marginal cost, its Lerner Index will be relatively low.
      (3) A monopoly restricts sales to raise its price above its marginal cost: the more inelastic is market demand, the higher a monopoly can raise its price above marginal cost.
   iv. It does not detect the power that a monopoly does not exercise. E.g., if a monopoly faces inelastic demand but nevertheless sets a price close to marginal cost, then the Lerner Index will be relatively low, indicating that the market is close to perfectly competitive.

8. Monopsony.

(a) Benefit and expenditure.
   i. Assumption: Maximization of net benefit.
   ii. Net benefit = benefit less expenditure.
   iii. Marginal benefit of a small quantity is very high and falls with the scale of purchases.
   iv. Price must be higher to induce a greater quantity of supply, so the average expenditure curve slopes upward.

v. The marginal expenditure is the change in expenditure resulting from an increase in purchases of one unit. For the average expenditure curve to slope upward, the marginal expenditure curve must lie above the average expenditure curve and slope upward more steeply.

(b) Maximizing net benefit.

i. The net benefit maximizing scale of purchases is where marginal benefit equals marginal expenditure.

ii. A monopsony restricts purchases (demand) to get a lower price and increase its benefit above the competitive level.

Answers to Progress Checks

8A. No difference: the price would be identical to the marginal revenue.

8B. It should raise price, so reducing sales up to the quantity where its marginal cost equals its marginal revenue.

8C. See figure 8C on page 449 of the textbook.

8D. The advertising expenditure should be $(140 – 70) × 0.01 × 1.4 = $0.98 million.

8E. If price and marginal cost increase by an equal percentage, then R&D expenditure should not change. If price and marginal cost increase by an equal dollar amount, then R&D expenditure should be reduced (the incremental margin will be lower).

8F. Lerner Index = (130 – 70)/130 = 0.46.

8G. Solar's total expenditure is represented by either the area u0vx under the marginal expenditure curve from a quantity of 0 to 6,000 tons or the rectangle t0vz.

Answers to Review Questions

1. (a) Star sports talent, such as Barry Bonds, gives the San Francisco Giants market power. (b) Microsoft's patents on the Windows operating system are a source of market power.

2. Economies of scale or scope give a firm a cost advantage over other sellers in the market. As the firm expands its production, its marginal costs will be lower than its competitors, enhancing its ability to price lower and gain even more sales, lowering cost further. Large economies of scale or scope will tend to cause the firm to dominate its market.

3. Lexus cars: high quality, particularly for customer service, permits Lexus to sell for a premium price, even compared with equivalent models manufactured by Toyota.

4. To sell additional units, a seller must reduce its price. So, when increasing sales by one unit, the seller will gain the price of the marginal unit but lose revenue on the inframarginal units. Hence, the marginal revenue is less than or equal to the price. If the demand is very elastic, then the marginal revenue will be close to the price. If, however, the demand is very inelastic, then the marginal revenue will be much lower than the price.

5. The publisher should reduce its price and sell additional units. For these units, the marginal revenue is greater than marginal cost, thereby increasing total profit. It should reduce price until the reduced marginal revenue becomes equal to the marginal cost.

6. True. The monopolist will only produce up to the point at which marginal revenue is equal to marginal cost – at this point, the price will exceed the marginal cost. In a competitive market, the equilibrium quantity would be where price equaled marginal cost. This would be at a greater quantity.
7. Expiration of the patent will (a) reduce Solar's market power; and (b) raise the price elasticity of demand.
8. The profit-maximizing quantity is such that the marginal revenue equals the marginal cost. Hence, after a change in costs, the seller should look for the quantity where the marginal revenue equals the marginal cost. So, it must consider both the marginal revenue and the marginal cost.
9. Advertising expenditure = (100 – 40) × 0.01 × 500,000 = \$0.3 million.
10. Raise advertising expenditure until the advertising-sales ratio equals the incremental margin multiplied by the advertising elasticity of demand.
11. Advertising elasticity would be higher for item (b).
12. Raise R&D expenditure until the R&D-sales ratio equals the incremental margin multiplied by the R&D elasticity of demand. Intuitively, the higher is the incremental margin and the more sensitive is demand to R&D expenditure, the more the business should spend on R&D.
13. A reduction in the degree of potential competition would lead to higher prices, thereby raising the Lerner Index for the industry.
14. True. The monopsony's marginal expenditure will exceed its average expenditure for an input, so by restraining purchases, the monopsony is able to obtain inputs for a lower price than if it equated average input price with its marginal benefit.
15. Hospitals with monopsony power will hire a quantity of nurses for which their marginal benefit exceeds the marginal supply price of the labor. This permits the hospital to offer lower wages. Therefore, there will be an excess demand at the wage rate that the hospital is willing to pay.

Sample Answer to Discussion Question

1. Eli Lilly owns the patent to Xigris, which at the time of writing, was the only approved drug for treatment of sepsis. Bayer manufactures aspirin, which is not covered by patent and is one of several drugs that relieve the symptoms of the common cold.
   (a) Who has relatively more market power: Eli Lilly over Xigris or Bayer over aspirin?
   (b) How is the difference between price and marginal revenue related to the price elasticity of demand?
   (c) Compare the difference between price and marginal revenue for the two drugs, Xigris and aspirin.

   Answer:

   (a) Persons suffering from sepsis do not have an alternative to Xigris. People suffering from the common cold can choose from many drugs including Bayer's aspirin. Accordingly, Eli Lilly has relatively more market power.
   (b) If the demand is very elastic, then the marginal revenue will be close to the price, and hence the difference between price and marginal revenue will be small. If, however, the

demand is very inelastic, then the marginal revenue will be much lower than the price, and hence the difference between price and marginal revenue will be large.

(c) The demand for Xigris is relatively inelastic by comparison with the demand for aspirin. Hence, the difference between price and marginal revenue will be greater for Xigris.

Chapter 9

Pricing

Chapter Summary

The simplest way to set price is through uniform pricing. At the profit-maximizing uniform price, the incremental margin percentage equals the reciprocal of the absolute value of the price elasticity of demand.

The most profitable pricing policy is complete price discrimination, where each unit is priced at the benefit that the unit provides to its buyer. To implement this policy, however, the seller must know each potential buyer's individual demand curve and be able to set different prices for every unit of the product.

The next most profitable pricing policy is direct segment discrimination. For this policy, the seller must be able to directly identify the various segments. The third most profitable policy is indirect segment discrimination. This involves structuring a set of choices around some variable to which the various segments are differentially sensitive. Uniform pricing is the least profitable way to set a price.

A commonly used basis for direct segment discrimination is location. This exploits a difference between free on board and cost including freight prices. A commonly used method of indirect segment discrimination is bundling. Sellers may apply either pure or mixed bundling.

Key Concepts

uniform pricing
price discrimination
complete price discrimination
segment
direct segment discrimination
free on board (FOB)
delivered pricing
cost including freight (CF)
indirect segment discrimination
bundling
cannibalization

General Chapter Objectives

1. Analyze uniform pricing and understand its limitations relative to price discrimination.
2. Analyze complete price discrimination and its implementation requirements.
3. Analyze direct segment discrimination and its implementation requirements.
4. Explain how location can be used as a basis for direct segment discrimination.
5. Analyze indirect segment discrimination and its implementation requirements.
6. Understand pure and mixed bundling, and when they should be applied.
7. Appreciate the hierarchy of pricing policies in terms of profitability and implementation requirements: (i) complete price discrimination; (ii) direct segment discrimination; (iii) indirect segment discrimination; and (iv) uniform pricing.
8. Understand that cost-plus pricing fails to maximize profit.
9. Appreciate how to manage cannibalization.

Detailed Notes

1. **Introduction.** Threads from previous chapters on demand, elasticity, costs, and monopoly are tied systematically to analyze how a seller with market power should set prices to maximize profit.

2. **Uniform pricing.**
   (a) Uniform pricing is a policy where a seller charges the same price for every unit of the product.
   (b) Price elasticity. Generally, if demand is inelastic, an increase in price will lead to a higher profit. Accordingly, a seller that faces an inelastic demand should raise the price.
   (c) Profit-maximizing price (incremental margin percentage rule) is where the incremental margin percentage (i.e., price less marginal cost divided by the price) equals the reciprocal of the absolute value of the price elasticity of demand. This is equivalent to the rule of marginal revenue equals the marginal cost.
      i. Determining the profit-maximizing price typically involves a series of trials with different prices as price elasticity may very along a demand curve and marginal cost may change with scale of production.
      ii. Intuitive factors that underlie price elasticity: availability of direct and indirect substitutes, buyers' prior commitments, search cost.
   (d) Demand and cost changes. Price adjustments following changes in demand and cost:
      i. To maximize profits, a seller should consider both demand and costs.
      ii. A seller should adjust its price to changes in either the price elasticity or the marginal cost.
      iii. It must consider the effect of the price change on the quantity demanded.
      iv. If demand is more elastic (price elasticity will be a larger negative number), the seller should aim for a lower incremental margin percentage, and not necessarily a lower price.

v. If demand is less elastic, the seller should aim for a higher incremental margin percentage, and not necessarily a higher price.
vi. A seller should not necessarily adjust the price by the same amount as a change in marginal cost.

(e) Common misconceptions/correct approach.
i. One should distinguish incremental margin percentage (i.e., price less average variable cost divided by the price) from contribution margin percentage (i.e., revenue less variable cost divided by revenue): Variable costs may increase or decrease with the scale of production, and hence, marginal cost will not be the same as average variable cost.
ii. A common mistake is the belief that the profit-maximizing price depends only on the elasticity. This approach considers only the demand and ignores costs. To maximize profits, however, management should take into account both the demand and costs.
iii. Cost-plus pricing (i.e., setting price by simply marking up average cost) will not maximize profit. Problems of cost plus pricing include:
(1) In businesses with economies of scale, average cost depends on scale, but sales and production scale depend on price. It is a circular exercise.
(2) Cost plus pricing gives no guidance as to the appropriate markup on average cost.

3. Complete price discrimination.

(a) Shortcomings of uniform pricing.
i. The inframarginal buyers do not pay as much as they will be willing to pay. A seller could increase its profit by taking their buyer surplus.
ii. An economically inefficient quantity of sales results. By providing the product to everyone whose marginal benefit exceeds marginal cost, the seller could earn more profit.

(b) Price discrimination.
i. Price discrimination is a policy where a seller sets different incremental margins on various units of the same or similar product.
ii. Complete price discrimination is the policy where a seller prices each unit at the buyer's benefit and sells a quantity such that the marginal benefit equals the marginal cost.

(c) Comparison with uniform pricing.
i. By pricing each unit at the buyer's benefit, the policy extracts all of the buyer surplus. Every buyer is charged the maximum she is willing for pay for each unit.
ii. The policy provides the economically efficient quantity; hence, it exploits all the opportunity for additional profit through increasing sales.
iii. Extracts a higher margin for units that would be sold under uniform pricing and extends sales by selling additional units that would not be sold with uniform pricing.

iv. To implement complete price discrimination, the seller must have information about each potential buyer's entire individual demand curve.

4. Direct segment discrimination is the policy where a seller charges a different incremental margin to each identifiable segment. A segment is a significant, cohesive group of buyers within a larger market.

(a) Homogeneous segments. For each segment, the profit-maximizing price is the buyers' willingness to pay (which is also their benefit from the item).

(b) Heterogeneous segments. If the buyers within each segment are heterogeneous and the seller lacks sufficient information to identify sub-segments, there are two alternatives:

i. Applying uniform pricing within each segment. Profit maximizing prices: Set prices so that the incremental margin percentage of each segment equals the reciprocal of the absolute value of that segment's price elasticity of demand; i.e., apply the rule for uniform pricing within each segment.

(1) Limitations. For each segment, same limitations as uniform pricing.

ii. Applying indirect segment discrimination within each segment.

iii. Implementation.

(1) The seller must identify and be able to use some identifiable and fixed buyer characteristic (e.g., age, gender, location) that segments the market.

(2) Must prevent buyers from reselling the product among themselves. Generally, resale of services is more difficult than resale of goods, hence it is easier to implement price discrimination in services than goods.

(3) Generally, with a policy of direct segment discrimination, prices should be set to derive a relatively lower incremental margin percentage from the segment with the more elastic demand and a relatively higher incremental margin percentage from the segment with the less elastic demand.

5. Location. To the extent that a product is costly to transport, a seller can discriminate on the basis of a buyer's location.

(a) FOB or CF.

i. A free on board (FOB or ex-works) price does not include delivery.

(1) FOB pricing ignores the differences between the price elasticities of demand in various markets.

(2) The differences among prices at various locations equal the differences in costs of delivery.

ii. Delivered pricing is the pricing policy where a seller's price includes delivery. A cost including freight (CF) price includes delivery.

(1) Assuming that the seller can prevent buyers in one country from reselling to buyers in the other country, the seller can implement direct segment discrimination across the two countries. This means

setting prices so that its incremental margin percentage in each country balances the reciprocal of the absolute value of the price elasticity of demand.

(2) The seller will aim for different incremental margin percentages in each market, and obtain higher profit. Then, it will be setting CF prices in the two markets; that is, prices including delivery, rather than FOB prices.

(3) The differences among prices at various locations are the result of the different incremental margin percentages and the different marginal costs of supplying the various markets, and may be larger or smaller than the freight costs. Depending on the price elasticities and the marginal costs, the difference may be larger or smaller than the freight cost.

(b) Restricting resale and managing the "grey market".

i. Customize product;

ii. Limit sales to markets where prices are low;

iii. Restrict warranty service to the country of purchase.

6. **Indirect segment discrimination** is the policy where a seller (who cannot directly identify the customer segments) structures a choice for buyers so as to earn different incremental margins from each segment.

(a) Structured choice. Indirect segment discrimination usually involves a structured choice that persuades the various buyer segments to identify themselves through their choices.

(b) Profit maximizing price.

i. There is no simple rule to find the profit maximizing prices.

ii. Buyers might substitute among the various choices. Accordingly, the seller must analyze how changes in the price of one product affect the demand for other choices, and set the prices of all products at the same time. The seller must not price any product in isolation.

iii. Ideally, the seller should design each of the alternative product choices to maximize the difference between the buyer's benefit and the seller's cost. The difference between the benefit and the cost is the maximum available profit.

(c) Implementation.

i. The seller must have control over some variable to which buyers in the various segments are differentially sensitive. The seller then uses this variable to structure a set of choices that will discriminate among the segments.

ii. Buyers must not be able to circumvent the differentiating variable. The seller must strictly enforce all conditions of sale to prevent switching.

7. Bundling.

(a) Bundling is one method of indirect segment discrimination that deliberately restricts buyer choices. This is the combination of two or more products into one package with a single price.

(b) Pure bundling is a pricing policy that offers only a bundle and does not allow the alternative of buying the individual products.

(c) Mixed bundling offers buyers a structured choice between the bundle and the individual products.

(d) Implementation. Bundling is more useful where:

 i. There is substantial disparity among the segments in their benefits from the separate products;

 ii. The benefits of the segments from the products are negatively correlated, i.e., a product that is more beneficial to one segment provides relatively little benefit to another;

 With (i) and (ii), the benefit from the bundle will be relatively less disparate across the segments than the benefits from the separate products; and

 iii. The marginal cost of providing each separate product is low (hence, relatively little economic inefficiency will accrue from providing the bundle to all buyers).

(e) When marginal cost is substantial, mixed bundling should be considered. By structuring a choice among the bundle and the separate products, various segments will identity themselves by their product choice. The economic inefficiency of providing a product for which the marginal cost is less than the buyer's benefit can be avoided.

8. Selecting the pricing policy.

Policy	Conditions	Profitability	Information requirement
Complete price discrimination	Seller discriminates directly on the buyer attributes. Seller can identify each buyer and charge different price for each unit.	Highest	The most
Direct segment discrimination	Seller discriminates directly on the segment attributes. Seller can identify each segment.	(Exception: When all buyers within each segment are identical, profit equals that with complete price discrimination.)	
Indirect segment discrimination	Uses product attributes to discriminate indirectly among various buyer segments.		
Uniform pricing		Lowest	The least

9. **Cannibalization.** When the sales of one product reduce the demand for another with a higher incremental margin.

   (a) Reason: the seller cannot discriminate directly, and must rely on a structured choice of products to discriminate indirectly. To the extent that the discriminating variable does not perfectly separate the buyer segments, cannibalization will occur.

   (b) Ways to mitigate cannibalization:
      i. Degrade low-margin item;
      ii. Use multiple discriminating variables to differentiate products;
      iii. Limit the availability of low-margin item.

Answers to Progress Checks

9A. The profit-maximizing price is 1,400 dirhams.

9B. The market buyer surplus is the area agc.

9C. Area adb = 2 million dirhams. Area bec = 2 million dirhams.

9D. See figure 9D on page 450 of the textbook.

9E. Japanese CF price = ¥50,000 = $500. The difference from the American price = $150.

9F. No, the two segments will not be differentially sensitive.

9G. Price the bundle at $22 and the educational channel at $19.

Answers to Review Questions

1. Not necessarily. The price also depends on the marginal cost.

2. The profit-maximizing uniform price = $2.50.

3. No.

4. Pricing books on based on the number of pages may approximate pricing based on production costs (assuming the marginal cost per page is reasonably constant), but will fail to account for demand conditions at all.

5. [Omitted].

6. Equal.

7. It would be easier to discriminate against newspapers because they have time value and are priced low relative to transportation cost.

8. The demand is relatively more price elastic in Singapore, so Microsoft should price with a lower incremental margin in Singapore.

9. [Omitted].

10. Current print subscribers will have a lower willingness to pay, since they already have access to the content of the publication.

11. Segments with higher demands (larger incremental margins) will want to consume more minutes. By offering plans containing different quantities of minutes, the providers induce buyers to self-select a package differentially designed for their willingness to pay.

12. Drivers who are on an expense account are not likely to care enough (i.e., they have a more inelastic demand) to spend the time to get gas at a nearby station, where it is cheaper. Thus, the higher price for gas from Hertz indirectly segments the market between those that are paying for themselves and those that are not.

13. The Economist comment points to segments with negatively correlated preferences. This is a condition under which bundling is especially profitable.

14. Pure bundling requires a buyer to purchase the bundle or not purchase any of its components: mixed bundling permits an option for consumers to purchase components of the bundle separately or together. In general, bundling is profitable when buyer tastes are negatively correlated across the components. Mixed bundling should be used when production is costly (so that it is not profitable to force buyers to purchase low-valued components) or when some buyers have extreme tastes (where some buyers have such a low value on one component of the bundle that the bundle price would need to be decreased too much in order to induce a sale to such buyers).

15. Cannibalization occurs when segments purchase products designed for other segments: that is, one product displaces sales of another with a higher incremental margin. It can be mitigated through product design (enhancing higher quality products or degrading lower quality products) or through limiting availability.

Sample Answer to Discussion Question

1. In September 2004, HSBC Holdings and Malayan Banking Berhad led a consortium of thirteen banks to provide a five-year US$200 million loan to Optimal Olefins. Optimal Olefins is owned by Petroliam Nasional Berhad, Dow Chemicals Company, and Sasol Limited of South Africa. The interest rate on the loan was set at the London Interbank Offer Rate (LIBOR) plus a spread of 44.5 basis points (0.445%). Banks source funds from demand, savings, and time deposits, as well as the interbank market. However, interest rates in the interbank market are usually higher than those on demand, savings, and time deposits. (Source: "HSBC, Maybank get 11 others to give Optimal US$468m loan", The Star Online, September 3, 2004.)

(a) Does LIBOR reflect a typical bank's average or marginal cost of funds?
(b) For purposes of pricing, which is relevant – average or marginal cost?
(c) What factors should banks take into account when setting the spread over LIBOR?
(d) Explain the banks' pricing policy in terms of the incremental margin percentage and the price elasticity of demand.

Answer:

(a) Since banks prefer to source funds from sources other than the London Interbank market, LIBOR reflects a bank's marginal cost of funds.
(b) For purposes of pricing, we need to know the marginal cost.
(c) The riskiness is one element of marginal cost. Banks should also consider the demand side, and specifically, the price elasticity.
(d) The spread, 0.445%, reflects the difference between price and the marginal cost for the loan (LIBOR plus an appropriate adjustment for risk). Then, 0.445%, when divided by the total interest rate on the loan, should be equal to the reciprocal of the absolute value of the price elasticity of demand.

Chapter 10

Strategic Thinking

Chapter Summary

In strategic situations, when the parties move simultaneously, there are several useful principles to follow: Avoid using dominated strategies, focus on Nash equilibrium strategies, and consider randomizing. When the parties move sequentially, a strategy should be worked out by looking forward to the final nodes and reasoning back to the initial node.

Through conditional or unconditional strategic moves, it may be possible to influence the beliefs or actions of other parties. In some settings, the first mover has the advantage; in others, the first mover is at a disadvantage. Finally, it is important to consider whether the situation will be played just once or repeated. The range of possible strategies is wider in a repeated situation.

In a zero-sum game, one party can become better off only if another is made worse off. In a positive-sum game, one party can become better off without another being made worse off.

Key Concepts

strategy
game theory
game in strategic form
dominated strategy
Nash equilibrium
randomized strategy
zero-sum game
positive-sum game
co-opetition
game in extensive form
backward induction
equilibrium strategy in a game in extension form
strategic move
first-mover advantage
conditional strategic move
threat
promise

General Chapter Objectives

1. Appreciate how game theory can guide strategic thinking in a wide range of situations.
2. Explain how the concept of Nash equilibrium predicts the outcome of strategic situations where parties act simultaneously.
3. Appreciate the use of randomized strategies, and calculate the Nash equilibrium in randomized strategies.
4. Distinguish strategic situations of competition and coordination.
5. Analyze strategic situations where parties act sequentially by backward induction.
6. Appreciate the use of strategic moves to influence the beliefs or actions of other parties.
7. Explain why conditional strategic moves are more cost-effective than unconditional strategic moves.
8. Understand how repetition expands the space of strategies and set of equilibria.

Detailed Notes

1. Introduction.

(a) A strategy is a plan for action in a situation where parties actively consider the interactions with one another in making decisions.
(b) Game theory is a set of ideas and principles that guides strategic thinking.
(c) The ideas and principles of game theory provide an effective guide to strategic decision making in many businesses.

2. Nash equilibrium.

(a) A game in strategic form is a tabular representation of a strategic situation, showing one party's strategies along the rows, the other party's strategies along the columns, and the consequences for the parties in the corresponding cells. This is a useful way to organize thinking about strategic decisions that parties must take simultaneously.
   i. A dominated strategy as one that generates worse consequences than some other strategy, regardless of the choices of the other parties. It makes no sense to adopt a dominated strategy.
   ii. Cartel's dilemma. A cartel is an agreement to restrain competition. Both companies know that, if they abide by their quotas, then they can increase their profit. However, when each individual company acts independently, it will decide to exceed its quota. The final outcome is that both companies exceed their quotas and erode the market price below the monopoly level.

(b) Nash equilibrium in a game in strategic form is a set of strategies such that, given that the other players choose their Nash equilibrium strategies, each party prefers its own Nash equilibrium strategy.
   i. A stable situation.

ii. In many typical strategic situations such as the cartel's dilemma, the Nash equilibrium strategies seem like the most reasonable and obvious way to behave.
iii. In others, such as the Battle of the Bismarck Sea, it is how the parties actually behaved.

(c) Solving the Nash equilibrium/equilibria.
i. The formal way.
(1) First, rule out dominated strategies; and
(2) Next, check the all the remaining strategies, one at a time;
or
ii. The informal "arrow" technique.
(1) A strategy is dominated if the row or column corresponding to the strategy has all arrows pointing out.
(2) If there is a cell with all arrows leading in, then the strategies marking that cell are a Nash equilibrium.

(d) Nonequilibrium strategies.
i. If one party does not adopt its Nash equilibrium strategy, then the best strategy for another party may or may not differ from the Nash equilibrium strategy.
ii. There may be no Nash equilibrium in pure strategies.

3. Randomized strategies.

(a) A pure strategy is one that does not involve randomization.
(b) A randomized strategy is a strategy for choosing among the alternative pure strategies in accordance with specified probabilities. The various probabilities must add up to 1.
(c) In each game in a strategic form, there will be a Nash equilibrium in either pure strategies or randomized strategies or both.
(d) In a competitive setting, the advantage of randomization comes from being unpredictable. If a party chooses in a conscious way, one party may be able to guess or learn the other party's decision and act accordingly.
(e) Solving for Nash equilibrium in randomized strategies.
i. Crossing point of lines representing the outcomes of alternative pure strategies as a function of the other party's probability; or
ii. Using algebra.

4. Competition or coordination.

(a) Competition.
i. A zero-sum game.
(1) This is a strategic situation where one party can be better off only if another is made worse off. A zero-sum game is the extreme of competition. There is no way for all parties to become better off.

(2) A strategic situation is a zero-sum when the consequences for the various parties add up to:
a. 0; or
b. the same number (whether negative, zero, or positive) in every cell of the game in strategic form.

ii. A positive-sum game.
(1) This is a strategic situation where one party can become better off without another being made worse off.
(2) The cartel's dilemma is not a zero-sum game. Rather, it is a positive-sum game.

(b) Coordination. If the two users can coordinate, both will benefit more. If, however, they fail to coordinate, both will benefit less. Strategic situations involving coordination are positive-sum games.

(c) Focal Point. By definition, Nash equilibrium strategies are self-enforcing in the sense that, if one party expects the others to follow their Nash equilibrium strategies, then its best choice is its own Nash equilibrium strategy. In situations of coordination, a Nash equilibrium provides a focal point for discussion and action by the two parties.

(d) Co-opetition is a strategic situation that involves elements of both competition and coordination.
i. E.g., the two TV stations would certainly cooperate to avoid the outcome where both schedule their news at the same time.
ii. The cartel's dilemma is a situation of co-opetition. Both sellers would like to cooperate and avoid production at the competitive level. The problem, however, is that following the quotas is a dominated strategy, and the result is that both exceed the quotas.
iii. Cooperation may arise when the strategic situation of co-opetition is repeated. By conditioning their actions on either external events or the previous actions of the other party, the parties involved may be able to avoid the undesirable outcomes of one-shot situations.

5. **Sequencing.** In many strategic situations, various parties move sequentially, rather than simultaneously.

(a) A game in extensive form is a graphical representation of a strategic situation, showing the sequence of moves and the corresponding outcomes. It consists of nodes and branches: a node represents a point where a party must choose an action, and the branches leading from a node represent the possible choices at the node.

(b) Backward induction.
i. This is a procedure for solving games in extensive form, looking forward to the final nodes and then reasoning backward toward the initial node.

(c) Equilibrium strategy.
i. Equilibrium strategy in a game in extensive form is a sequence of the best actions, where each action is decided at the corresponding node.

ii. It is different from that of the Nash equilibrium strategy in a game in strategic form. In a strategic form, the parties act simultaneously, and a party's Nash equilibrium strategy is the best strategy given that the other parties adopt their respective Nash equilibrium strategies.

(d) Uncertain consequences.

i. In uncertain circumstances, even if one party does not know the consequences of the various actions for the other party, it may know or be able to assess the probabilities with which the other party will choose between the alternative actions. It can apply backwards induction using these probabilities.

6. Strategic Moves.

(a) A strategic move is an action to influence the beliefs or actions of other parties in a favorable way.

i. Typically involves self imposed restrictions and real costs; e.g., destroying the lithograph plates.

(b) Credibility. A strategic move must be credible to be effective. Credibility may depend on sunk investments or other commitments.

(c) A first mover advantage gives a party an advantage if it moves before others.

i. To identify whether a strategic situation involves first mover advantage, it is necessary to analyze the game in extensive form.

ii. First mover advantage is not a universal rule in business or other strategic situations. In some circumstances, the follower has an advantage, e.g., in retail pricing.

7. Conditional strategic moves.

(a) A conditional strategic move is an action under specified conditions to influence the actions or beliefs of other parties in a favorable way.

i. Conditional strategic moves are more cost-effective than unconditional strategic moves.

(b) There are two types of conditional strategic moves.

i. Threats. A threat imposes costs under specified conditions; e.g., poison pill, strikes.

ii. Promises. A promise conveys benefits under specified conditions, e.g., deposit insurance.

8. Repetition.

(a) With repeated interaction, a party may condition its actions on external events or the actions of other parties.

i. The range of possible strategies is much wider in repeated interactions than in one-shot scenarios. In situations that involve coordination, the wider range of strategies may enable the various parties to achieve better outcomes than in interactions that occur only once.

(b) Conditioning on External Events. In the context of the battle for the evening news, a station could adopt a strategy under which its schedule is conditioned on some independent variable, e.g., the alternating strategy will be better than fighting over the 8:00 p.m. slot on a once only basis, which might result in both stations broadcasting their news at the same time.

(c) Conditioning on Other Parties' Actions. Such strategies can improve the outcome in the context of the cartel's dilemma.

i. In a once-only cartel, individual members have an overwhelming incentive to exceed their quotas.

ii. In a repeated cartel, a seller can adopt a strategy under which it conditions its production on the actions of another party at an earlier time.

(1) A tit-for-tat strategy combines a promise with a threat. The promise is to follow the quota if the other seller follows its quota. When all sellers follow their quotas, they can achieve profits above the competitive level. The threat is to produce more than one's quota if the other seller exceeds its quota. Whenever a seller exceeds its quota, it will depress the market price and, hence, reduce the profits of other sellers.

(2) Whether a tit-for-tat is an equilibrium strategy for all parties in the repeated cartel depends on two factors.

a. The rate of discounting future cash flows.

b. The likelihood that the cartel will be terminated in the future due to the obsolescence of the product or entry of new competitors.

iii. In a cartel that extends to several markets, the tit-for-tat strategy promises a greater benefit: increased profit in all the markets if sellers restrict production. Moreover, the tit-for-tat strategy threatens a greater punishment: reduced profit in all the markets if sellers exceed their quotas.

Answers to Progress Checks

10A. A presidential election candidate must consider how other candidates will react to her or his decisions. Accordingly, these decisions are strategic.

10B. See figure 10B on page 451 of the textbook.

10C. (1) If Ming prices high, its expected profit would be (40,000 2/5) + (40,000 3/5) = 40,000.
(2) If Ming prices low, its expected profit would be (50,000 2/5) + (30,000 3/5) = 38,000.

10D. It is not a zero-sum game.

10E. See figure 10E on page 451 of the textbook. Delta would choose 7:30 p.m.

10F. See figure 10F on page 452 of the textbook. Agua Luna would produce 2 million bottles, and Moonlight would produce 1 million bottles.

10G. Minimum probability is 2/10 = 1/5.

Answers to Review Questions

1. (c).
2. A dominated strategy is a strategy that yields a poorer outcome regardless of what the other player(s) choose. A Nash equilibrium is a set of strategies such that if each other player follows their equilibrium strategies, then it is best for a player to follow their equilibrium strategy. This holds true for all players.
3. (c).
4. Venus chooses Orange with probability 0.5 and chooses Green with probability 0.5; and Sol does the same.
5. (b).
6. If your boyfriend chooses to look in location A, then it will be optimal for you to look in location A. This is true for every location in the store. The customer service counter is a focal point because it is sensible that you and your boyfriend would want to discuss which of the many Nash equilibria to choose – the particular location matters less than the agreement to go to the same location.
7. Yes – any gain of one party of x means that the other party's gain is −10 – x.
8. Venus will choose either Orange or Green – either way, it will receive 1.5. Please refer to figure 10RQ8 on page 452 of the textbook.
9. [Omitted].
10. Strategy (b) is more credible.
11. The strategy may not be internally consistent, in the sense that, if and when a party reaches a particular node, he/she may prefer to take some action other than that in the planned strategy. Generally, there is no way to choose the best strategy at any node without looking at the entire sequence of potential moves after that point – essentially this means using backward induction.
12. Conditional strategic moves may be less costly.
13. [Omitted].
14. Legal loans have the threat of legal action to induce recipients to repay their loans. In the absence of legal sanctions, some other credible threat must be found. Violence is used to make the threat credible.
15. In repeated situations, strategies may be conditioned on external events or the actions of other parties.

Sample Answer to Discussion Question

1. The National Collegiate Athletic Association (NCAA) restricts the amount that colleges and universities may pay their student athletes. Suppose that there are just two colleges in the NCAA – Ivy and State. Each must choose between paying athletes according to NCAA rules or paying more.
   (a) Construct a game in strategic form to analyze the choices of Ivy and State.
   (b) Identify the equilibrium/equilibria.
   (c) The NCAA rules have government backing. How will this affect the equilibrium or equilibria?

   Answer:

   (a) The key to this question is constructing the game in strategic form. The NCAA functions as a buyer cartel in the market for college athletes. If both Ivy and State pay according to NCAA rules, then they succeed as a cartel – they receive 3 each. If Ivy breaks the cartel and pays more, while State keeps to the cartel, then Ivy will benefit and State will lose – Ivy gets 4, and State gets 1. Similarly, if Ivy keeps to the cartel and State breaks it, Ivy gets 1 and State gets 4. Finally, if they both pay more, then both will be worse off – each receives 2.

		State College	
		Pay by NCAA rule	Pay more
Ivy College	Pay by NCAA rule	I: 3, ↓ S: 3 →	I: 1, ↓ S: 4
	Pay more	I: 4, S: 1 →	I: 2, S: 2

(b) The Nash equilibrium is both colleges will pay more than the NCAA allows.

(c) If the NCAA has government backing, then both colleges will follow the NCAA recruiting rules, and achieve the highest combined profit.

Chapter 11

Oligopoly

Chapter Summary

Prices are strategic complements. In an oligopoly, where sellers compete on price, if one seller raises or lowers its price, then others will adjust prices in the same direction. Sellers can dampen price competition by differentiating their products.

Production capacities are strategic substitutes. In an oligopoly, where sellers compete on production capacity, if one seller raises or lowers capacity, then, others will adjust capacities in the opposite direction.

If a seller can commit to its production capacity before others, then it will gain a first-mover advantage. If the leader commits to sufficient production capacity, it can even exclude all potential entrants.

Competing sellers can increase profit by restraining competition – either through agreement or horizontal integration. Antitrust (competition) authorities consider the industry Herfindahl–Hirschman Index in deciding whether to investigate mergers.

Key Concepts

Bertrand model
Hotelling model
best response function
strategic complements
Cournot model
residual demand curve
strategic substitutes
Herfindahl–Hirschman Index (HHI)
limit pricing
Stackelberg model
cartel
horizontal integration
vertical integration
antitrust (competition) policy

General Chapter Objectives

1. Introduce oligopoly as a market structure.
2. Study oligopoly in the short run – how competing sellers set price and how their pricing depends on whether the product is homogeneous or differentiated, and how each seller should adjust price in response to competitors' price changes.

3. Study oligopoly in the long run – how competing sellers decide on production capacity and how each seller should adjust capacity and production in response to competitors' changes in capacity and production.
4. Understand that competing sellers/buyers can raise profit by restraining competition among themselves.
5. Apply the analyses of oligopoly to antitrust law and policy, the aim being to regulate competition.

Detailed Notes

1. **Introduction.** Oligopoly is a market structure that lies between the two extremes of perfect competition (no seller has market power) and monopoly (there is only one seller).
   (a) A market is an oligopoly if it comprises a small number of sellers, whose actions are interdependent.
   (b) A market is a duopoly if it comprises two sellers.

2. **Pricing (assuming that the various sellers move simultaneously).**
   (a) Homogeneous product.
      i. In the **Bertrand** model of oligopoly, sellers which produce at constant marginal cost with unlimited capacity compete on price to market a homogeneous product. (The monopoly maximizes profit at the scale of operations where the marginal revenue equals marginal cost.)
      ii. In the context of a duopoly, the market equilibrium is perfectly competitive pricing.
         (1) Any higher price would induce the other seller to alter its strategy.
         (2) The price cutter faces a demand curve that it is infinitely elastic.
      iii. This ruinous competitive outcome is essentially the Prisoners' dilemma. Oligopolistic competitors can avoid this through repeated competition.
         (1) Sellers may adopt "tit-for-tat" strategies – price high, observe competitors' pricing, and cut price only if the competitor cuts price.
         (2) "tit-for-tat" may be a Nash equilibrium. The oligopolists would succeed in avoiding price wars and achieve tacit (not explicit) cooperation.
   (b) Differentiated product.
      i. In the **Hotelling** model of duopoly, sellers which produce at constant marginal cost with unlimited capacity compete on price to market products differentiated by their distance from each consumer's ideal preference.
      ii. The profit-maximizing price would be a function of a seller's own marginal cost, the other seller's price, and the consumers' transport cost (disutility for difference from her ideal preference).

(1) With differentiation, the price-cutter's demand is not infinitely elastic. If one seller cuts its price below the competitor's price, it would take away only part of the competitor's entire demand.

iii. In the context of price competition between oligopolists, a seller's best response function shows its best action as a function of competing sellers' actions. Through product differentiation, sellers can avoid ruinous price competition.

(1) Greater transport costs (preference differences) cause the products to be more differentiated and the demand to be less price elastic, hence the equilibrium price exceeds marginal cost and would be higher.

(2) As transport costs (preference differences) approach zero, the Nash equilibrium price would approach marginal cost. This is the outcome with homogeneous products and with perfect competition. With zero transport costs (preference differences), product differentiation no longer pays.

(c) Product design (location of product in space of consumer preferences).

i. There is no position that all consumers prefer.

ii. Managers must balance their desire for market share (locating close to their customers) with their wish to avoid head-to-head price competition.

(1) The less differentiated the products, the more direct is price competition, and the lower would be incremental margins.

(2) However, when differentiation moves the seller's product too far away from the buyers' preferences, the seller risks losing too much of the market (sales) to competitors.

(d) Strategic complements.

i. Actions by various parties are strategic complements if an adjustment by one party leads other parties to adjust in the same direction.

ii. Prices are strategic complements in the following settings:

(1) In price competition between oligopolists with unlimited capacity that offer differentiated products (Hotelling model);

(2) In price competition between oligopolists with unlimited capacity that offer homogeneous products (Bertrand model).

3. Capacity (assuming that the various sellers move simultaneously).

(a) In the long run, the strategic variable for oligopolistic sellers is production capacity. It is assumed that, under all market structures, sellers plan capacity exactly equal to the expected scale of production, hence "capacity," "scale," and "production" are treated as synonymous.

i. In the Cournot model of oligopoly, sellers which produce at constant marginal cost compete on production capacity to market a homogeneous product.

(1) A seller's residual demand curve is the market demand curve less the quantities supplied by other sellers. Using its residual demand

curve, a seller can calculate its profit-maximizing capacity by equating its residual marginal revenue with the marginal cost.

(2) To find the Nash equilibrium in capacities, we must calculate the sellers' respective best response functions. The Nash equilibrium of the oligopolistic situation is at the intersection of the two best response functions.

ii. The market price is established at a level that equates the market demand with the total production capacity offered.

iii. The total capacity with duopoly is less than that under perfect competition, while the market price under duopoly is higher than that under perfect competition.

(b) Cost differences.

i. The best-response functions do not depend on the seller's fixed costs. Any change in fixed costs will not affect the sellers' choices of capacity and the market equilibrium.

(c) Multiple sellers.

i. When there are multiple sellers with differing marginal costs, the Nash equilibrium of the best response functions can be written in a way that relates the incremental margin (price relative to marginal cost) percentage to:

(1) market demand elasticity; and

(2) a measure of industry concentration.

ii. Intuitively, the more concentrated is the industry, and the more inelastic is the market demand, the higher would be the incremental margin percentage.

iii. In a market characterized by a Cournot model, as the number of sellers in the market increases:

(1) the total capacity increases; and

(2) the market price decreases.

iv. The **Herfindahl–Hirschman Index** (HHI) measures industry concentration as the sum of the squares of the various sellers' market shares.

(1) A monopoly would have a market share of 100%, so, the HHI would be $(100)^2$ or 10,000.

(2) In a perfectly competitive industry, each of the many sellers would have almost zero market share, so, the HHI would be close to zero. HHIs exceeding 1,800 are generally viewed as representing significant market concentration.

(3) The HHI is usually reported in terms of percentage points.

(d) Strategic substitutes.

i. Actions by various parties are strategic substitutes if an adjustment by one party leads other parties to adjust in the opposite direction.

ii. In the Cournot model of competition between oligopolists on production capacity, capacities are strategic substitutes.

iii. Generally, whether strategic variables are strategic complements or strategic substitutes depends on the relevant demand and cost conditions.

(1) Advertising and R&D expenditure may be either strategic complements or strategic substitutes.
(2) Increased R&D spending can have a similar effect to increasing capacity.
(3) On the other hand, an increase in one producer's R&D expenditure may drive competitors to increase R&D as well, particularly when they compete for patents.

4. Price/Capacity Leadership. Sequential actions present the possibilities of first mover advantage and strategic moves. We must consider the actions and consequences in sequence, and apply the concept of equilibrium in a game in extensive form.

(a) Price.
  i. Limit pricing is a strategic move by which an industry leader commits to a level of production so high that any entrant cannot make a profit, and so, will not enter the industry.
  ii. The market price is established at the level that equates the market demand with the total industry (leader plus follower) production.
  iii. The leader can control the residual demand curve facing the entrant.
    (1) The leader need only produce a quantity sufficient to position the entrant's residual demand curve so that it lies below (to the left of) the entrant's average cost.
    (2) This first-mover advantage – being able to forestall entry – depends on two factors.
      a. The leader's first move is viewed as a commitment that will not be reversed regardless of the entrant's actions.
      b. Production involves a fixed cost. If there were no fixed cost, then the entrant's average cost curve would slope upward throughout. Then, however large is the leader's production, the entrant would profit from entry to produce at some scale of production, albeit very low.

(b) Capacity.
  i. In the long-run, the leader must take account of the entrant's production capacity. In the **Stackelberg model** of oligopoly, which is the sequential version of the **Cournot model**, the leader commits to capacity before the follower, and both sellers produce at constant marginal cost and market a homogeneous product.
  ii. The market price is established at the level that equates the market demand with the total industry (leader plus follower) production capacity.
  iii. When deciding its production capacity, the leader takes account of the entrant's subsequent choice of production capacity.
    (1) The follower fares worse despite its better information because the leader is committed to its production capacity.

iv. Oligopoly markets where sellers are differentiated, have different cost structures, and dynamically adjust their strategies are complicated to model.

5. **Restraining competition.** A monopoly is more profitable than an oligopoly – whether the businesses compete on price or capacity. An oligopoly is at least as profitable as a perfectly competitive industry. Rather than compete, sellers can increase profits by restraining competition among themselves. Competing sellers can restrain competition in two ways: through agreement or by integration.

(a) Cartels.

i. A buyer cartel is an agreement among buyers to restrain competition in demand.

ii. A seller cartel is an agreement among sellers to restrain competition in supply

(1) A seller cartel sets a maximum sales quota for each participant. By limiting each participant's sales, the cartel restricts the quantity supplied and raises sellers' profit above the competitive level.

(2) The key to an effective cartel is enforcement against:

a. Existing sellers exceeding their quotas; and

b. The entry of new competitors.

(b) Enforcement. The effectiveness of private enforcement depends on several factors.

i. The number of sellers in the market. A cartel will be more effective in an industry with relatively few sellers than in a fragmented industry.

ii. The relation of industry capacity to market demand. If all sellers are operating near capacity, it will be difficult for them to expand and little incentive to exceed the specified quotas.

iii. The extent of sunk costs. Sellers with significant sunk costs will be relatively more willing to cut price and exceed their quotas.

iv. The extent of barriers to entry and exit.

v. The nature of the product – homogeneous or heterogeneous – has an ambiguous influence on the effectiveness of a cartel.

(c) Labor unions.

i. Unions are explicit seller cartels.

ii. Negotiations in which workers are represented by a union are called collective bargaining.

iii. A union with a closed shop in a particular business has a monopoly over the labor supply to that business.

(d) Horizontal integration.

i. Horizontal integration is the combination of two entities, in the same or similar businesses, under a common ownership.

(1) The horizontal integration of any two businesses with market power will lead to a reduction in the quantity supplied, raise the market price and increase profits, subject to the entry of potential competitors.

ii. Vertical integration is the combination of the assets for two successive stages of production, under a common ownership.

6. Antitrust (competition) policy.

(a) Competition laws.

i. Antitrust (competition) policy aims to ensure a degree of competition that maximizes social welfare.

ii. Generally, competition laws prohibit the following:

(1) Competitors from colluding on price and other means;

(2) Monopolies and monopsonies from abusing market power;

(3) Mergers or acquisitions that would create monopolies or monopsonies; and

(4) Specific anticompetitive business practices such as control over resale prices and exclusive agreements.

iii. Enforcement involves two dimensions:

(1) Prosecution against those who violate the laws; and

(2) Review proposals for mergers and acquisitions.

(b) Merger guidelines.

i. A crucial step in determining the competitive impacts of a merger is the definition of the market. This is defined as a product or group of products and a geographic area in which a hypothetical profit-maximizing firm could impose a "small but significant and non-transitory" increase in price. The relevant market is no bigger than what is necessary to satisfy this test.

ii. Antitrust authorities consider the HHI, along with information about cost efficiencies, innovative effects, and other strategic and dynamic factors.

(1) Increases in industry concentration (as measured by the HHI) are directly related to the extent to which price exceeds marginal cost.

(2) A merger that increases the HHI and potentially decreases the merged firm's costs, has two of the major ingredients relevant to an antitrust investigation.

Answers to Progress Checks

11A. See figure 11A on page 453 of the textbook.

11B. See Figure 11B on page 453 of the textbook.

11C. When one of the companies increases R&D, does the other company respond by increasing its R&D (strategic complements) or decreasing it (strategic substitutes)?

11D. No, it also depends on their relative costs and whether or not their product is differentiated from that of other sellers. It also depends on the potential competition available from sellers not currently in the market – if they can enter easily, then the seller may not be dominant, regardless of its size relative to the other sellers presently in the market.

11E. The union will be more effective the less available is non-unionized labor in the industry. It will be more effective the less available additional workers are, and the less feasible it is for current workers to expand their hours (i.e., their capacity). Sunk costs, in the form of specialized training, will make unions less successful (other things being equal). On the other hand, any barriers to entry or exit (such as specialized training) will tend to make unions more effective. Finally, the more homogeneous the labor (repetitive easily monitored tasks), the more effective the union.

11F. Horizontal integration combines two entities that are selling similar products while vertical integration combines two entities that sell different stages in the production of a single product.

11G. If the merger were to reduce costs significantly, consumers may benefit from a merger that substantially increases concentration. Also, if a merger creates a more viable competitor for other significantly larger sellers in the market, it may become more competitive even while the measure of market concentration increases.

Answers to Review Questions

1. False. For example, price should equal marginal cost under Bertrand competition even in a duopoly.
2. Higher.
3. Shortening the distance between the sellers is the same thing as decreasing product differentiation in the market. The result should be lower prices, and possibly lower consumer benefits (if the differentiation was valuable to consumers).
4. Raise your level of that action.
5. Strategic substitutes mean that if a competitor does more of an activity, then you should do less.
6. It would reduce the potential competition by eliminating each as a potential entrant into the other's market.
7. If there are no fixed costs, then it is not possible for the dominant firm to choose a price below the minimum average cost point of a potential competitor. That is, there is no price that will preclude entry, since entry will not involve any fixed cost.
8. You should choose a relatively larger capacity if you can precommit.
9. The number of sellers in the market, the relation of industry capacity to market demand, the extent of sunk costs, the extent of barriers to entry and exit, and the nature of the product (degree of homogeneity).
10. A cartel is easier to enforce with less heterogeneity since it is easier to monitor the sales of the sellers. On the other hand, if the product is less heterogeneous, the demand facing each individual seller is more elastic, and so, they will have more incentive to cut price.
11. (a) 5000; (b) 6250.
12. Suppose that all sellers but one have negligible market shares. The one big seller would have a market share of 31.6% (the square root of 1,000).
13. HHI = 3333. Markup is 16.67%.
14. The Department of Justice and the Federal Trade Commission.
15. Merger Guidelines are used to determine when a proposed merger must be more fully examined before being approved. They include, among other factors, consideration of the post-merger level of the HHI in an industry, and how much the HHI changes as a result of the merger.

Sample Answer to Discussion Question

1. As an analyst of the media industry, consider the extent to which you would apply the Hotelling model of oligopoly to competition between newspapers in any city that are differentiated by:

(a) The degree of local, national, and international news coverage;
(b) Political positioning – liberal vis-à-vis conservative;
(c) Timeliness of sports news;
(d) Layout – color vis-à-vis black-and-white.

Answer:

In the Hotelling model, capacity is not an issue, sellers are differentiated by their "distance" from consumers' tastes, consumer marginal "travel costs" are constant, and consumer tastes are distributed relatively uniformly. This would seem to apply reasonably to (a) and (b): some would like more local coverage, while others would prefer more international coverage; some are liberal while others are conservative. The Hotelling model would not apply to (c). There is no reader segment that prefers less timely sports coverage. Similarly, the Hotelling model would not apply to (d). Probably all readers prefer color to black-and-white.

Part III

Imperfect Markets

Chapter 12

Externalities

Chapter Summary

An externality rises when one party directly conveys a benefit or cost to others. A network externality arises when a benefit or cost directly conveyed to others depends on the total number of other users. An item is a public good if one person's increase in consumption does not reduce the quantity available to others. Equivalently, a public good provides nonrival consumption.

The benchmark for externalities and public goods is economic efficiency. At that point, all parties maximize their net benefits. Externalities can be resolved through unilateral or joint action, but resolution may be hampered by differences in information and free riding. Similarly, the commercial provision of a public good depends on being able to exclude free riders. Excludability depends on law and technology.

Markets with network effects differ from conventional markets in several ways. Demand is insignificant until a critical mass of users is established. Expectations of potential users help to determine the attainment of critical mass. When the demand for competing services is close to critical mass, a small shift in demand towards one service can tip all other users toward that service.

Key Concepts

externality
public good
positive externality
negative externality
externality is resolved
free rider
network effect
network externality
critical mass
installed base
tipping
nonrival
rival
congestible
excludable
patent
copyright

General Chapter Objectives

1. Understand positive and negative externalities, and their economically efficient level.
2. Explain why it is profitable to resolve externalities, and how to do so.
3. Appreciate how information and free-riding can impede resolution of externalities.
4. Identify network effects and externalities and apply the concept to the Internet and e-commerce.
5. Distinguish the managerial implications of markets with network externalities from conventional markets.
6. Discuss the concept of a public good and its economically efficient level.
7. Examine the role of technology and law in excluding users from a public good.

Detailed Notes

1. Introduction.

(a) An externality arises when one party directly conveys a benefit or cost to others.
   i. A positive externality arises when one party directly conveys a benefit to others, e.g., additional business generated by a new store to the existing shops.
   ii. A negative externality arises when one party directly imposes a cost to others, e.g., business taken away by a new store from existing shops.

(b) An item is a public good if one person's increase in consumption does not reduce the quantity available to others, e.g., fireworks. Public goods can be privately provided.

2. Benchmark.

(a) An externality conveys a benefit or cost directly rather than through a market.

(b) Positive externalities. In deciding on the levels of activities that give rise to externalities:
   i. If the source considers only the benefits and costs to itself, and ignores the benefits and costs to others, i.e., ignoring the externalities.
      (1) To maximize profit, it should invest up to the point that the marginal benefit equals marginal cost.
      (2) At this level of investment, however, it may be ignoring opportunities for additional profit from positive externalities.
   ii. Considering the benefits of an externality to the group (all possible recipients):
      (1) The group marginal benefit curve from an externality is the vertical sum of the individual marginal benefits.
      (2) If one party generates positive externalities, the group maximizes profit at the level of investment where the group marginal benefit equals the marginal cost of the activity generating the externality.

(c) Negative externalities. Considering the costs of an externality to the group (all possible recipients)
   i. The group marginal cost from an externality is the vertical sum of the individual marginal costs.
   ii. If one party generates negative externalities, the group maximizes profit at the level of investment where the marginal benefit from the activity generating the externality equals the group marginal cost.

(d) Externalities in general.
   i. If one party generates both positive and negative externalities, the group maximizes profit at the following benchmark: where the sum of the marginal benefits equals the sum of the marginal costs.
      (1) This defines the economically efficient level of the activity generating the externalities.
      (2) This is the point where an externality is resolved.
   ii. Suppose the sum of marginal benefits exceed the marginal cost of a positive externality, there is a profit opportunity for an intermediary to collect fees from the recipients (up to their respective marginal benefits) to pay the source (an amount sufficient to cover the source's marginal cost) to increase the externality to the economically efficient level.
   iii. Similarly if the marginal benefit falls short of the sum of marginal costs of a negative externality, there is a profit opportunity for an intermediary to collect fees from the recipients (up to their respective marginal costs) to pay the source (an amount sufficient to cover the source's marginal benefit) to reduce the externality to the economically efficient level.
   iv. The same benchmark applies when the source of the externality is separate from or integrated with the recipients.
   v. To take account of non-monetary externalities, we require the recipients to measure the benefits and costs in terms of money and suppose that, rather than maximizing profit, these recipients aim to maximize their net benefit, which is the benefit less the cost.

3. Resolving externalities.

(a) This involves deliberate action as externalities do not pass through markets.

(b) Practical ways to resolve externalities.
   i. Merger of the source and the recipient of an externality into a single entity.
      (1) Once the source and recipient of the externality are combined, no matter who acquires whom, the single entity will take account of all benefits and costs of its investments and invest up to the economically efficient level (group marginal benefits equal group marginal costs).
   ii. Joint action. Where merger is not feasible:
      (1) The source and recipient of the externality could negotiate and agree to resolve the externality (while remaining separate entities).

(2) They collect information on the benefits and costs to the various parties and plan the level of activity that generates the externality.
   a. In the case of a positive externality, the recipient will pay the source (a contribution equal to the recipient's marginal benefit from the activity generating the externality) to increase the source's investment.
   b. E.g., In the case of positive externalities, the source will maximize profit by choosing the level of activity where the sum of marginal benefits equals the marginal cost.

(3) Then, they must enforce the agreed plan: monitoring the source and applying incentives to ensure that the source complies with the planned level of the externality-generating activity.

(c) Free rider problem. Informational differences and free riders hamper the resolution of an externality.
   i. A free rider is a party that contributes less than its marginal benefit to the resolution of the externality.
   ii. In the extreme, the free rider avoids all contribution.
   iii. It may be costly to exclude certain parties from receiving a benefit, especially when the externality affects many recipients and the recipients differ widely in their marginal benefits.

4. Network effects and externalities.

(a) Introduction.
   i. A network effect arises when a benefit or cost depends on the total number of other users.
      (1) The adjective "network" emphasizes that the effect is generated by the entire network of users, e.g., connections to telephone service generate network effects.
      (2) The marginal benefit and demand for an item that exhibits network effects depends on the total number of other users in addition to price, buyer income, and prices of related products.
   ii. A network externality is a network effect that is conveyed directly and not through a market.
      (1) The benchmark for an activity that exhibits network externalities is economic efficiency: the sum of marginal benefits equals the sum of marginal costs.
   iii. The presence of network effects or network externalities implies that the character of demand and competition will differ from that in conventional supply–demand markets.

(b) Critical mass. In markets with network effects, demand is zero unless the number of users exceeds the critical mass.
   i. Critical mass is the number of users at which the quantity demanded becomes positive.

   ii. If each user needs one separate unit of the complimentary hardware, an alternative way to measure the size of the critical mass is the size of the installed base, which is the quantity of the complementary hardware in service.

(c) Expectations. Expectations of potential users help to determine the attainment of critical mass. Expectations can be influenced through commitments and hype.

(d) Tipping.
   i. Tipping is the tendency for the market demand to shift toward a product that has gained a small lead in total number of users.
   ii. In markets with network effects, where demand is close to the tipping point (near critical mass), demand is extremely sensitive to small differences among competitors.
      (1) If demand for some product just exceeds critical mass, any slight movement in demand away from that product will tip all the users away.
   iii. In a market for competing products that generate network effects, the likelihood of tipping means that one product may dominate the market.

(e) Price elasticity. The presence of network effects affects the price elasticity of demand.
   i. When market demand is below critical mass, demand is zero, and extremely price inelastic.
   ii. When demand exceeds critical mass, the network effect tends to amplify the effect of a price change on quantity demanded and causes demand to be relatively more elastic.

5. Public goods.

(a) A public good provides nonrival consumption. There is an extreme economy of scale in providing a public good. Provision involves only a fixed cost and the marginal cost of serving additional consumers or users is zero.

(b) Rivalness. There is a continuum between nonrival, congestible, and rival consumption.
   i. Consumption is nonrival if one person's increase in consumption does not reduce the quantity available to others, i.e., a public good (such as fireworks).
   ii. Consumption is congestible if one person's increase in consumption by some quantity reduces the total quantity available to others but by less than that quantity. Congestible items are public goods when consumption is low but are private goods when consumption is high, e.g., Internet service, transportation facilities.
   iii. Consumption is rival if one person's increase in consumption reduces the total available to others by the same quantity, i.e., a private good (such as food and clothing).

(c) Content vis a vis delivery.
   i. Content is always nonrival.
   ii. Delivery method may be a public good (e.g., delivery of TV by over the air transmission) or a private good (e.g., delivery of TV via cable).

(d) Economically efficient level of public good: at the point where the sum of individual marginal benefits equals the marginal cost. Opportunities to profit from adjusting provision are exhausted at that point.

6. **Excludability.** The basis for commercial provision of many public goods is to deliver them in the format of private goods.

(a) Consumption is excludable if the provider can exclude particular consumers.
(b) Excludability is a fundamental condition for the commercial production of any product. Otherwise free riders will cut into the seller's revenues, profits and hamper provision.
(c) Excludability depends on law and technology.
   i. Law – establishes excludability through intellectual property:
      (1) Patent: a legal, exclusive right to a product or process (associated with scientific knowledge).
      (2) Copyright: a legal, exclusive right to an artistic, literary or musical expression.
   ii. Enforcement. The owner of a copyright or patent can sue the infringers for a court order to stop the infringement as well as an award of damages. Enforcement cost varies with product.
   iii. Note that law varies with time and among legal jurisdictions.
(d) Excludability also depends on technology, e.g., scrambling technology, access technology, e.g., passwords.

Answers to Progress Checks

12A. Same as figure 12.1, except that the group marginal benefit is the same as Luna's marginal benefit. The profit-maximizing investment is now $900,000.

12B. (1) Sol's marginal cost curve will be higher, and (2) the level of investment that maximizes the group profit will be lower. Please refer to figure 12B on page 454 of the textbook.

12C. Transactions costs (information, monitoring, and enforcement). Also, the parties must be convinced that the potential benefits of joint action exceed the private benefits available through free-riding.

12D. (a) is a network externality; (b) is not a network externality, as the benefit is limited to the neighborhood.

12E. See figure 12E on page 455 of the textbook.

12F. See figure 12F on page 455 of the textbook.

Answers to Review Questions

1. [Omitted].
2. The sum of the marginal benefits must equal the marginal cost.
3. The amount that the recipients of the negative externality are willing to pay for a marginal reduction is less than or equal to the marginal cost. The amount that the source is willing to accept for a marginal reduction is greater than or equal to the marginal benefit. Since the sum of the marginal costs exceeds the marginal benefits, the intermediary could make money.
4. (a) The subway system will now consider the benefits to users of land around the subway line and should invest to the point that the sum of the marginal benefits to all of its uses equals the marginal cost.
   (b) As part owners of the subway system, the adjacent landowners will have incentives to promote additional investment by the subway system beyond what would benefit only the subway system itself.
5. The motel understands that if the exit gets built, it will reap the benefits whether it has contributed to the cost or not. It cannot be excluded from benefiting, as long as the exit is built.
6. Videoconferencing systems are more valuable the more users there are (in the limit of one user, there is no value). There may not be sufficient demand to cover the costs unless there is a critical mass of users that provides enough value. If a new technology were to become available and were to gain sufficient users, the network could tip from the old technology to the new fairly easily.
7. A user interacts directly with their network browser and uses it to access web pages – any browser is capable of reaching the same web pages. Hence, there is little value to be gained by using the same browser as others. Indeed, on the Internet, nobody knows what browser you are using.
8. Relatively more price elastic near the tipping point; relatively less price elastic when the demand is far from the tipping point.
9. Technical standards are more important in markets with network effects because compatibility creates value for the users. Absent network effects, there is little value to compatibility so standards do not matter to individual users (since the standards do not lead to compatibility that has any value).
10. [Omitted].
11. (a) but not (b).
12. Since public good consumption is nonrival, whatever quantity is provided to one consumer is provided to all consumers (at least, those that cannot be excluded). Since they are all consuming the same quantity of the public good, the marginal benefit to the group is the sum of the marginal benefits to the individuals.
13. The law creates legal exclusive rights such as copyright and patent. Technology can change the method of access to an item from excludable to non-excludable.
14. Patents and copyright both create legal exclusive rights. Patents apply to products or processes, while copyright applies to artistic, literary, or musical expressions.
15. [Omitted].

Sample Answer to Discussion Question

1. A study of leasing practices among U.S. shopping malls reported that, on average, department stores paid rent of $2.24 per square foot. After controlling for differences in sales per square foot among stores of different types, the study calculated that the average rent for a specialty store was $11.88 per square foot. (Source: B. Peter Pashigian and Eric D. Gould, "Internalizing Externalities: The Pricing of Space in Shopping Malls", Journal of Law and Economics, Vol. 41 No. 1 (April 1998), 115–142.)

(a) Compare the development of new department store along an open street with one in a shopping mall. In which case are the externalities more likely to be resolved?

(b) Explain why shopping malls charge department stores much lower rent than specialty retailers.

(c) Explain why shopping malls might charge specialty stores a variable rent that depends on sales revenue.

Answer:

(a) Within the mall. The mall owner can encourage positive externalities and discourage negative ones.

(b) The department stores attract shoppers who then also patronize specialty stores within the mall. The department stores are called anchor tenants. For economic efficiency, they should be paid for generating positive externalities. This is reflected in their lower rent.

(c) It is difficult to exclude shopping mall stores from benefits associated with investment in the mall. Thus, the total value of any investment will be the sum of the benefits to all mall occupants. Specialty stores are likely to differentially benefit from any particular investment (e.g., an electronics store will benefit more from convenient parking than will a toy store). By charging variable rent that depends on sales revenue, the mall is attempting to recover these varying benefits that accrue to the individual stores in the mall. Sales revenue is an imperfect, but easily verified, measure of individual store benefits from the mall.

Chapter 13

Asymmetric Information

Chapter Summary

In situations of asymmetric information, the allocation of resources will not be economically efficient. The asymmetry can be resolved directly through appraisal or indirectly through screening, signaling, or contingent payments. The indirect methods depend on inducing self-selection among parties with different characteristics. Screening is an initiative of the party with less information, while signaling is an initiative of the party with better information.

A key business application of screening is indirect segment discrimination in pricing. A related application is auctions, which exploit strategic interaction among competing bidders to force bidders with higher values to pay higher prices.

When the distribution of information is asymmetric, one or more parties will have imperfect information and hence bear risk. The distribution of risk may conflict with the self-selection needed to resolve the asymmetric information.

Key Concepts

asymmetric information
imperfect information
risk
risk averse
risk neutral
insurance
adverse selection
screening
self-selection
reserve price
discriminatory auction
nondiscriminatory auction
winner's curse
signaling
contingent payment

General Chapter Objectives

1. Understand the concepts of imperfect information, risk, and asymmetric information.
2. Appreciate the managerial implications of adverse selection, and, specifically, the possibility of market failure.

3. Analyze how asymmetric information can be resolved through appraisal.
4. Analyze how asymmetric information can be resolved through screening.
5. Discuss two specific applications of screening – indirect segment discrimination and auctions.
6. Analyze how asymmetric information can be resolved through signaling.
7. Analyze how asymmetric information can be resolved through contingent payment.
8. Apply the theory of asymmetric information to lending and insurance markets.

Detailed Notes

1. **Asymmetric information.** In a situation of asymmetric information, one party has better information than another, e.g., credit, labor, antiques, and insurance markets.

2. **Imperfect information.**
   (a) Imperfect information vis-à-vis asymmetric information.
      i. Imperfect information.
         (1) Imperfect information is the absence of certain knowledge by a single person or by more than one party.
         (2) A market can be perfectly competitive even when buyers and sellers have imperfect information, so long as they all have symmetric but imperfect information.
         (3) In a perfectly competitive market, the forces of demand and supply will channel resources into economically efficient uses; no further profitable transactions are possible.
      ii. Asymmetric information.
         (1) Asymmetric information involves two or more parties, one of whom has better information than the other or others.
         (2) Asymmetric information will always be associated with imperfect information, because the party with poorer information definitely will have imperfect information.
         (3) A market where information is asymmetric cannot be perfectly competitive. If buyers and sellers can resolve the information asymmetries, they can increase their benefits by more than their costs.
   (b) Risk defined. Risk is uncertainty about benefits or costs and arises whenever there is imperfect information about something that affects benefits or costs.
      i. A person can have imperfect information about something, but if that thing does not affect her/his benefits or costs, it does not impose any risk on her/him.
   (c) Risk Aversion.
      i. A risk averse person prefers a certain amount to risky amounts with the same expected value.

ii. A risk-neutral person is indifferent between a certain amount and risky amounts with the same expected value.
iii. Insurance is the business of taking certain payments in exchange for eliminating risk.

3. Adverse selection.

(a) Adverse selection arises in situations of asymmetric information.
  i. In an adverse selection, the party with relatively poor information draws a selection with relatively less attractive characteristics.

(b) Demand and supply, market equilibrium and economic inefficiency.
  i. The equilibrium in a market with asymmetric information will not be economically efficient. For example, when fakes are introduced in an antiques market:
    (1) Each buyer purchases up to the point where its actual marginal benefit (adjusted down for the probability of getting a fake) balances the market price. Each legitimate seller supplies up to the point where its marginal cost balances market price.
    (2) Buyers who get genuine items have a marginal benefit higher than the legitimate sellers' marginal cost. Buyers who get fakes have a marginal benefit less than the legitimate sellers' marginal cost.
  ii. At equilibrium, marginal benefit does not equal marginal cost.
    (1) The quantity traded is not economically efficient.
    (2) Effect on buyer's surplus is ambiguous. Buyer surplus falls as some buyers get fakes. Buyer surplus rises as market price falls and sales are higher.
    (3) Legitimate sellers get a lower price and sell fewer units. Sellers of fakes are the only ones that are better off.
  iii. Sellers of fakes impose a negative externality on buyers and legitimate sellers.
  iv. By resolving the negative externality (information asymmetry), benefits will increase by more than costs, and a profit can be made.

(c) Market failure.
  i. Severe adverse selection can cause a market to fail, and price changes do not help to restore equilibrium. For example, when fakes are introduced in an antiques market:
    (1) Antiques buyers with less information draw a mixture of fakes and genuine antiques, which is an adverse selection of items.
    (2) As market price drops, legitimate sellers supply a smaller quantity. Quantity of fakes is not affected, increasing the proportion of fakes, leaving buyers with a worse adverse selection. A price reduction cuts demand and supply and does not necessarily restore the equilibrium.
    (3) In the extreme, so many fakes flood the market that actual demand curve drops to zero and the market fails (there is no sale at all).

(d) Lending and insurance.
   i. Lending. To the extent that borrowers have better information about their personal willingness to default, there is asymmetric information between borrowers and lenders. Generally, a lender will have some chance of lending to a (bad) borrower who would readily default and some chance of lending to a (good) borrower who would be reluctant to default. If the lender raises the interest rate, it will draw an adverse selection of borrowers: the higher the interest rate, the fewer good borrowers will want loans and the higher will be the proportion of bad borrowers.
   ii. Insurance. If an insurer charges a high premium, it is likely to draw applicants who know that they are in relatively poor health or who maintain risky lifestyles.

4. Appraisal.

(a) Appraisal works only if:
   i. The characteristic about which information is asymmetric is objectively verifiable.
   ii. The potential gain (for buyer: difference between marginal benefit and market price; for seller: difference between market price and marginal cost) covers the cost of appraisal. This, in turn, depends on two factors. One is the proportion of fakes. The other is the difference between the marginal benefit and the marginal cost.

(b) Procuring the appraisal. Seller should procure the appraisal when:
   i. There are many potential buyers;
   ii. Various potential buyers seek the same information.

(c) Appraising borrowers. Appraisal (including credit checks, employment records in the lending market) can directly resolve asymmetric information, e.g., Moody's appraisals.

5. Screening.

(a) Screening is the initiative of a less-informed party to indirectly elicit the other party's characteristics, e.g., points in home mortgages, physical examinations for life insurance applicants.
   i. Screening is an indirect way to resolve asymmetric information.
   ii. Screening works only if the less informed party can identify and control some variable to which the better-informed parties are differentially sensitive.
      (1) The less informed party must design choices around that variable to induce self-selection.
      (2) In self-selection, parties with different characteristics choose different alternatives.
   iii. Indirect segment discrimination is an application of screening to pricing. A seller who is less informed about how much the buyer is willing to pay

for an item uses indirect segment discrimination to induce self-selection among buyers with different price elasticities of demand.

(b) Differentiating variable(s).

i. When the less-informed party has the choice of several differentiating variables, it should structure the choice that drives the biggest possible wedge between the better-informed parties with the different characteristics.

ii. The less-informed party must consider the effectiveness of each differentiating variable in driving a wedge between the various segments by comparing the differential sensitivity of the segments to each variable. It should place relatively more emphasis on the more effective variable.

iii. The most effective screening may involve a combination of the differentiating variables (e.g., to screen between leisure vis-à-vis business travelers, airlines use restrictions, advance booking, weekend stay-over, frequent flyer points).

(c) Multiple unobservable characteristics.

i. If a party is uninformed about several characteristics, then screening based on a single differentiating variable may not resolve the asymmetry.

ii. To resolve information asymmetries through screening, the less-informed party needs as many differentiating variables as there are characteristics that it cannot observe (e.g., (i) driver's carefulness, (ii) degree of risk aversion).

6. Auctions.

(a) Auctions are another application of screening.

i. A seller who doesn't know buyers' valuations can use an auction to sell, while a buyer doesn't know sellers' costs can use an auction to buy.

ii. An auction applies competitive pressure to the participating bidders. Each bidder must act strategically since its best bid depends on the competing bids. Each bidder faces a fundamental trade-off. By bidding more aggressively, it will improve its chances of winning the auction but will get a smaller profit from winning the auction.

iii. The differentiating variable in an auction is the probability of winning. Thus, the auction induces self selection among the participants according to their respective values for the item.

(b) Auction methods.

i. Open auction. The bidders in an open auction can see each other's behavior. Colluding bidders can observe whether they are each abiding by their collusive agreement.

(1) The seller in open auction can counteract collusion by applying a reserve price. The reserve price is the price below which the seller will not sell the item.

(2) In setting a reserve price, the seller must balance the increased revenue from a sale against the probability of no sale: when there

are many bidders, it is more likely that at least one bidder will exceed the reserve price.

ii. Sealed-bid auction. In a sealed-bid auction, a bidder can easily cheat on the collusive agreement with a bid exceeding the agreed price.

iii. In a discriminatory auction, each winning bidder pays the price that she or he bid.

iv. In a nondiscriminatory auction, each winning bidder pays the price bid by the marginal winning bidder.

(1) Bidders make relatively higher bids in nondiscriminatory auctions.

(2) Sellers' revenues in a nondiscriminatory auction may or may not be higher. A seller collects only the price bid by the marginal bidder.

(c) Winner's curse.

i. The winner's curse is that the winning bidder over-estimates the true value of the item for sale.

ii. The winner's curse is more severe when:

(1) Number of bidders is larger,

(2) True value of the item is more uncertain, and

(3) In a sealed-bid as compared with open auction – since the record of bidding is open, the price at which a bidder drops out reveals information about her estimate of the true value of the item. The remaining bidders can use this additional information to refine their estimate of the true value. Hence, open bidding mitigates the winner's curse.

iii. When the winner's curse is more severe, a bidder should bid more conservatively.

7. Signaling.

(a) Signaling is an action initiated by the better-informed party to communicate its characteristics in a credible way to the less-informed party.

i. It is an indirect way to resolve asymmetric information.

(b) Credibility.

i. Signaling is credible only if it induces self-selection among the better-informed parties (e.g., buy back offers by sellers of genuine antiques).

ii. Costless signaling is not credible.

iii. The cost of the signal must be sufficiently lower for parties with superior characteristics than for parties with inferior characteristics.

(c) Advertising and regulation. Three conditions for advertising to be a credible signal of product quality:

i. Investment must be sunk (e.g., reputation built up over a long time): a reversible investment is not credible.

ii. Buyers must be able to detect poor quality relatively quickly.

iii. The word of poor quality must spread and cut into the seller's future business.

8. Contingent payment.

(a) Definition: a payment made if a specific event occurs, e.g., bets.
  i. An indirect way to resolve asymmetric information.
  ii. Induces self-selection among the better-informed parties (e.g., sellers offering products of different quality).
  iii. May serve as screens (e.g., a potential buyer could take the initiative of offering the seller a choice between payment in a share of the production or straight cash) or signals (e.g., selling a plantation for a share of the production).

(b) Insurance compensation is a contingent payment, e.g., in the event of death or illness.

Answers to Progress Checks

13A. Nancy has imperfect information but does not face risk. The insurer has imperfect information and faces risk.

13B. The market price will be higher, as shown in figure 13B on page 456 of the textbook.

13C. The percentage of high-risk policyholders will fall.

13D. Appraisals will be more common in the market for more expensive antiques.

13E. Borrowers who are more willing to repay will be relatively more likely to post collateral.

13F. (a) It should provide the information to the bidders. (b) This information will reduce the extent of the winner's curse.

13G. Screening is an initiative of the less-informed party, while signaling is an initiative of the better-informed party.

Answers to Review Questions

1. Imperfect information is the absence of certain knowledge. Risk is uncertainty about benefits or costs. A person can have imperfect information about something, but if that thing does not affect her/his benefits or costs, it does not impose any risk on her/him.

2. (a) No asymmetry. (b) The directors of Acquirer have better information than the general investor.

3. (a) True. (b) False. Risk neutral persons will not want insurance.

4. Yes, this will draw relatively less hard-working persons.

5. The seller has an interest not to reveal negative information about the car.

6. [Omitted].

7. Drivers with a higher probability of accident will prefer a lower deductible as they are more likely to make a claim.

8. Drives whose value of time is less than the toll will not pay, and hence be screened away in favor of those whose value of time exceeds the toll.

9. (a) Open bidding allows the participants to observe the bids of others. This supports collusion. (b) Setting a reserve price will put a limit to collusion.

10. (b).

11. [Omitted].

12. Yes.

13. Borrowers who post collateral are less likely to default. The collateral serves as a screening mechanism.

14. A contingent payment is a payment that only takes place when specific conditions occur, as with an insurance payment that occurs only when a specified loss condition takes place.

15. By accepting payment in Acquirer's shares, the amount that Target receives will depend on Target's true value.

Sample Answer to Discussion Question

1. Southwest Airlines pioneered the concept of a low-cost airline, operating from secondary airports with short hops and quick turn-arounds. Unlike the major U.S. network carriers, Southwest has succeeded in being consistently profitable for three decades. In 2005, Southwest increased net income by 75.1% to $548 million, or by 76.3% to $0.67 per share. One reason for Southwest's financial performance despite the sharp spike in the price of oil is that in 2005, the airline had hedged 85% of its fuel requirements at $26 per barrel of crude oil. Hedging saved the airline almost $900 million. Table 13.2 reports selected financial and operating information.

(a) Referring to Southwest's fuel consumption in 2005. Explain how a 10-cent increase in the price of jet fuel would affect Southwest's costs and income.

(b) Southwest is averse to risk. Explain why it has purchased crude oil derivatives to hedge the price of jet fuel.

(c) Suppose that the actual price of crude oil turns out to be lower than the price at which Southwest hedged. Was Southwest wrong to have hedged?

Table 13.2 Southwest Airlines

	2005	2004
Total operating revenues ($ million)	7,584	6,530
Operating income ($ million)	820	554
Net income ($ million)	548	313
Available seat miles (billions)	85.2	76.9
Average fuel cost (cents per gallon)	103.3	82.8
Fuel consumed (million gallons)	1,287	1,201

Answer:

(a) Since 85% of the fuel costs had been hedged, the 10 cent increase in fuel price would only have increased fuel costs by 0.15 × 10 cents per gallon × 1,287 million gallons, or $19.305 million. This would reduce net income by only 3.5%, despite a fuel price increase of 9.7%.

(b) The crude oil derivatives meant that rises in crude oil prices would have a reduced impact on Southwest's net income. Conversely, reductions in crude oil prices would also have a reduced impact on Southwest's net income. As a result, Southwest willingly gave up potential cost savings in exchange for reduced exposure to potential cost increases, as risk averse decision makers should.

(c) Southwest would not experience much of a cost decrease, but this does not make it a mistake. The hedge was a form of insurance. It obtained the benefits of insurance against potential oil price increases even if oil prices actually fell.

Chapter 14

Incentives and Organizations

Chapter Summary

The architecture of an organization comprises the distribution of ownership, incentive schemes, and monitoring systems. Ownership means the rights to residual control. Incentive schemes and monitoring systems are related as incentives must be based on behavior that can be observed. An efficient incentive scheme balances the incentive for effort with the cost of risk.

An efficient organizational architecture resolves four internal issues – holdup, moral hazard, monopoly power, and economies of scale and scope. Holdup and moral hazard arise between parties with a conflict of interest. Additionally, moral hazard depends on one party not being able to observe the actions of the other. Holdup can also be resolved through more detailed contracts, moral hazard through incentive schemes and monitoring systems, and internal monopoly power through out-sourcing.

Key Concepts

organizational architecture
moral hazard
performance pay
performance quota
relative performance
holdup
specificity
complete contract
ownership
residual control
residual income
vertical integration

General Chapter Objectives

1. Discuss the problem of moral hazard.
2. Analyze monitoring systems and incentive schemes to resolve moral hazard.
3. Appreciate the risk imposed by incentive schemes.
4. Understand how to give incentives for multiple responsibilities.
5. Discuss the problem of holdup and how it can be mitigated through complete contracts.

6. Analyze how vertical integration affects the potential for holdup, degree of moral hazard, monopoly power, and economies of scale and scope.
7. Discuss the problem of internal monopoly power and how it can be mitigated through outsourcing.
8. Discuss the design of organizational architecture.

Detailed Notes

1. Organizational architecture.

(a) Organizational architecture comprises the distribution of ownership, incentive schemes, and monitoring systems. The vertical and horizontal boundaries of the organization are two implications of the organizational architecture.

(b) An efficient organizational architecture revolves and should be designed to balance four internal issues:

i. holdup;
ii. moral hazard;
iii. monopoly power; and
iv. economies of scale and scope.

2. Moral hazard.

(a) Moral hazard exists when one party's actions affect but are not observed by another party with whom it has a conflict of interest, e.g., delivery persons, sales representatives, and senior management in large publicly listed corporations are subject to moral hazard.

(b) Asymmetric information about actions. Moral hazard arises when there is asymmetric information about some future action of the better-informed party.

(c) Economic efficiency. The relevant parties would like to resolve the moral hazard so that the better-informed party will make the economically efficient choice.

i. The degree of moral hazard is measured by the discrepancy between the actual effort and the economically efficient level.
ii. Economically efficient level of effort:
(1) Employer's benefit = revenue – other costs – wages and other incentives paid to the worker subject to moral hazard.
(2) Worker's net benefit = wages and incentives – cost of effort.
(3) Group's net benefit from the worker's effort = employer's benefit – worker's cost of effort.
(4) Employer's marginal benefit from the worker's effort = change in employer's profit from worker's increase in effort.
(5) Worker's marginal cost of effort = additional cost required to increase effort.
(6) Economic efficiency for the group: level of worker's effort where employer's marginal benefit balances worker's marginal cost.

iii. The actual action or effort chosen by a party subject to moral hazard will diverge from the economically efficient level.
   (1) Worker acts independently and considers only her personal marginal benefit and marginal cost from effort, not the employer's marginal benefit.
   (2) The worker chooses the level of effort that balances her personal marginal benefit with her marginal cost.
   (3) The lower the worker's marginal benefit relative to the employer's marginal benefit, the lower the effort the worker chooses relative to the economically efficiency level.

(d) The degree of moral hazard is the difference between the economically efficient action and the action chosen by the party subject to moral hazard. The larger this difference, the greater will be the degree of moral hazard and the gain in net benefit that can be realized by resolving the moral hazard.

3. Incentives.

(a) There are two complementary approaches to resolve moral hazard: monitoring systems and incentive schemes.

(b) Monitoring. The simplest monitoring system (e.g., time clock, vehicle log, random checks by supervisors, customer reports) focuses on objective measures of performance.

(c) Performance pay.
   i. Incentive schemes align incentives of the party subject to moral hazard with those of the less-informed party by tying payments to some observable measure of performance.
   ii. They depend on:
      (1) A link between the unobservable action and some observable measure of performance.
      (2) What observable measures are available, i.e., information provided by monitoring systems.
   iii. Performance pay is an incentive scheme that bases pay on some measure of performance (e.g., a commission per delivery).
      (1) An incentive scheme is relatively stronger (resulting in higher level of worker's effort) if it provides a higher personal marginal benefit for effort.

(d) A performance quota is a minimum standard of performance (set to achieve the economic efficient level of effort), below which penalties (e.g., deferral of promotion, pay reduction, dismissal) apply.
      (1) A performance quota is cost effective. It does not reward effort below or above the economically efficient level.

(e) Multiple responsibilities. A party may be subject to moral hazard with respect to multiple responsibilities, i.e., when one party's multiple actions (as opposed

to a single action) affect but are not observed by another party with whom it has a conflict of interest.
   i. An incentive scheme should balance the multiple responsibilities: monitoring each of the unobservable actions and with incentives based on each of the corresponding indicators.
   ii. An incentive scheme that focuses on one responsibility may aggravate moral hazard associated with other functions.
   iii. When there are responsibilities for which it is difficult to measure performance, a deliberate use of weak incentives is a way to achieve the appropriate balance among responsibilities.

4. Risk.

(a) Risk arises whenever incentives are based on an indicator that depends on extraneous factors (e.g., monthly sales revenue depends also on the general state of the economy, traffic, weather, customers' orders, etc.) and the party subject to moral hazard has imperfect information about those extraneous factors.
   i. An economically efficient scheme (one that maximizes net benefit) must balance the incentive for effort with the cost of risk.

(b) Costs of risk. The costs of risk depend on 3 factors:
   i. The structure of the incentive scheme: the stronger the scheme, the higher the risk on the party subject to moral hazard;
   ii. The degree of risk aversion of the party subject to moral hazard: the more risk averse that the party is, then the larger will be the cost imposed by risk; and
   iii. The effect of the uncertain extraneous factors: if the indicator is sensitive to these factors and the factors are subject to wide swings, the risk will be higher.
      (1) Stronger schemes should be adopted when the party subject to moral hazard is relatively less risk averse and the extraneous factors are stronger.

(c) Relative performance incentives. Incentive schemes based on relative performance (e.g., fixed pay plus a commission for all sales revenue above an average level) are an effective way of reducing risk due to common extraneous factors.
   i. Effect of common extraneous factors is cancelled out to the extent they affect all workers equally (e.g., a bad economy).

5. Holdup.

(a) Holdup is an action intended to exploit another party's dependence.
   i. Like moral hazard, it arises only when there is a conflict of interest between the parties.
   ii. Distinct from moral hazard, it does not require asymmetric information.
   iii. The prospect of a holdup leads other parties to take precautions (to avoid dependence) which either reduce the benefit from the relationship or increase costs, reducing the group's net benefit.

(b) Specific investments.
   i. The specificity of an investment in an asset is the percentage of the investment that will be lost if the asset is switched to another use.
   ii. The costs of holdup will be higher if the relevant assets are more specific.
   iii. The prospect of holdup deters investments in all forms of specific assets (e.g., physical assets and human capital).

(c) Incomplete contracts. A complete/more detailed contract would resolve holdup, but would be very costly to prepare.
   i. A complete contract specifies what each party must do and the corresponding payments under every possible contingency.
   ii. The degree to which a contract should be incomplete depends on:
      (1) The potential benefits and costs at stake; and
      (2) The extent of possible contingencies.

(d) Gains form resolution. A profit can be made by resolving the potential for holdup.

6. Ownership.

(a) Residual income. Another way to resolve holdup is through changing the ownership of the relevant assets.
   i. Ownership means the rights to residual control (those rights that have not been contracted away). Rights to residual control include:
      (1) The right to receive residual income from the asset (i.e., the income remaining after the payment of all other claims) and the benefit of changes in income and costs.
   ii. A transfer of ownership means shifting the rights of residual control to another party.

(b) Vertical integration. Vertical integration is the combination of the assets for two successive stages of production under a common ownership.
   i. Downstream: closer to the final consumer.
   ii. Upstream: further from the final consumer. The "make or buy" decision is a decision to vertically integrate upstream.
   iii. Vertical integration changes ownership of assets and alters the rights to residual control and residual income.
   iv. It affects the degree of moral hazard and resolves holdup.

7. Organizational architecture.

(a) Implications.
   i. The architecture of the organization comprises the distribution of ownership, incentive schemes, and monitoring systems. Vertical and horizontal boundaries are just two implications of the architecture of the organization.
   ii. The design of organizational architecture depends on a balance among four issues – holdup, moral hazard, internal monopoly, and scale and scope economies.

(b) Holdup. Holdup can be resolved by changing the ownership of relevant assets (e.g., holdup by a delivery service can be resolved by vertical integration into the delivery business).

(c) Moral hazard. Vertical integration increases the degree of moral hazard. The internal supplier is subject to moral hazard. Giving ownership to the worker will resolve the moral hazard.

(d) Internal monopoly. The internal supplier may acquire monopoly power. The organization should outsource (purchase services or supplies from external sources) whenever the internal provider's cost exceeds that of external sources.

(e) Economies of scale and scope. The internal supplier may lack economies of scale and scope as compared with external suppliers.

   i. The external contractor would have better capacity utilization and hence a lower average cost. It would be less costly to purchase the service from the external contractor.

   ii. Economies of scope are the major factor in favor of wide horizontal organizational boundaries. If the company already produces one item, it can reduce total cost by producing the other one as well. However, if the company does not already produce either item, then economies of scope imply that it should outsource both.

(f) Balance. The decision on organizational architecture depends on a balance among: the scope for holdup, the degree of moral hazard, internal monopoly power, and the extent of economies of scale and scope. It also depends on other ways to resolve these issues.

Answers to Progress Checks

14A. The new marginal cost curve lies above the original. Please refer to figure 14A on page 457 of the textbook. (a) The economically efficient effort will be lower. (b) The effort that the worker actually chooses will be lower.

14B. Draw any personal marginal benefit curve that crosses the marginal cost curve at 120 units of effort.

14C. See figure 14C on page 457 of the textbook.

14D. The sales clerk's incentive to process returns will be reduced.

14E. Marie's.

14F. On-the-job training.

14G. SBC and Amgen integrated downstream. China National Petroleum Company integrated upstream.

14H. The potential to reduce holdup through detailed contracting; the potential to resolve moral hazard through incentives and monitoring; the potential for outsourcing to reduce internal monopoly power; and the extent of economies of scale for the internal group.

Answers to Review Questions

1. [Omitted].
2. Regarding asymmetry, it is costly for the insurer to monitor Leah's precautions. There is a conflict of interest because, with insurance, Leah bears the cost of precautions but receives only part of the benefit.
3. When moral hazard exists, one party will invest less than is efficient in some costly activity. That is, they will stop investing when their marginal benefit is equal to the marginal cost. However, the marginal benefit to the other party will be greater than the party doing the investing. Thus, by resolving the moral hazard, the marginal benefits to the other party will exceed the marginal costs to the investing party, with potential profits for both.
4. Method (b) provides more incentive to the lawyer.
5. The drivers can be rewarded for breakdown expenses below the average for all drivers and penalized for breakdown expenses above the average.
6. The scheme will reduce the secretary's incentive for effort in the other tasks.
7. (a) Index of small stocks; (b) Index of U.S. government bonds; (c) Index of Japanese stocks.
8. (b).
9. Because the additional cost of preparing a complete contract outweighs the potential benefit in avoidance of holdup.
10. (i) Shareholders have residual control (rights that have not been contracted away). For instance, they may dismiss the current board of directors and management. (ii) Shareholders also have the rights to residual income (income remaining after the payment of all other claims). They receive dividends only after all other claims, such as interest and trade debts, have been paid.
11. [Omitted].
12. False. It would resolve the potential for holdup, but increase moral hazard by the internal producer of avionics.
13. If the internal supplier quotes a price that is too high, internal customers will outsource. This constrains the monopoly power of the internal supplier.
14. For: reduces potential for hold up. Against: increases moral hazard, creates internal monopoly, and does not benefit from scale economies.
15. Economies of scope are one reason for horizontal integration: the organization can produce a variety of products at lower cost than if each item were produced separately. However, if the organization produces none of the items for which there are economies of scope, then it should outsource all of them rather than producing a small subset. If production of an item is subject to economies of scale, then if two producers merge (integrating horizontally), they can lower their average production cost.

Sample Answer to Discussion Question

1. CapitalMall Trust is a real estate investment trust that owns and manages the IMM Building, a Singapore shopping mall. Until 2004, tenants of the IMM Building paid a fixed monthly rental. Then, for new or renewed tenancies, CapitalMall set a two-part rental, comprising a fixed monthly payment of S$35–38 (Singapore dollars) per square foot and a variable payment of up to 1% of the tenant's gross revenue. The new tenancies last for two years. When tenants complained about the variable payment, CapitalMall asserted that it was a common

practice that helped to align the interests of landlord and tenant. ("Seeing RED over RENT", Straits Times, October 20, 2004, H24.)

(a) As manager of the IMM Building, how is CapitalMall subject to moral hazard with respect to its tenants?
(b) How would the variable payment align the interests of landlord and tenant?
(c) How should the variable payment depend on the landlord's attitude towards risk?
(d) Should the variable payment be based on the tenant's gross revenue or net revenue (gross revenue less cost of goods sold)?

Answer:

(a) CapitalMall is responsible for activities – security, maintenance, parking – that affect the number of customers that visit the mall. The tenants cannot directly monitor these efforts. CapitalMall incurs the costs of these activities, while the tenants enjoy the benefits, hence there is a conflict of interest. Thus, CapitalMall is subject to moral hazard.
(b) The variable payment means that tenants with more customers and presumably, higher revenues, would pay higher rents. Hence, CapitalMall would be rewarded for attracting more customers. Thus, the interest of CapitalMall and the tenants would be aligned.
(c) Suppose that the landlord is risk-averse. If its costs of security, maintenance, parking, etc. are fixed, it would prefer fixed rental payments rather than variable rental payments. If its costs vary with the number of customers, then it would prefer variable rental payments tied to the number of customers.
(d) The revenue is an indicator for the maintenance costs imposed by a tenant's customers. If it is the number of customers that matters, then the variable payment should be based on net revenue. However, maintenance expenses may also be caused by the items a store is selling (e.g., heavy durable goods may impose higher costs for the mall operator). In that case, gross revenues would be a better indicator of maintenance expenses caused. One reason to base the variable rental on gross rather than net revenue is practical: it is easier to monitor gross revenues than net revenues – because the tenant may inflate its reported costs, and so, reduce its reported net revenue.

Chapter 15

Regulation

Chapter Summary

The marginal benefit of an item may diverge from the marginal cost for three basic reasons: market power, asymmetric information, and externalities and public goods. This divergence results in economic efficiency. Government regulation may help where private action fails to resolve the economic inefficiency.

Generally, the government can regulate the conduct, information, and structure of an industry. Specifically, the conduct of a franchised monopoly may be regulated directly through price or indirectly through the rate of return. Competition law regulates the conduct and structure of businesses in general. In situations of asymmetric information, mandatory disclosure is one form of regulation.

Externalities may be regulated through fees or standards. The efficient degree of an externality depends on location and time. The government can help to resolve inefficiency in accidents and public goods by providing an appropriate legal framework. The laws regarding copyrights and patents must balance the incentive for new research against inefficient use of existing knowledge.

Key Concepts

natural monopoly
privatization
marginal cost-pricing
average cost pricing
rate base
self-regulation
law of torts
liability

General Chapter Objectives

1. Analyze how government regulation can resolve the economic inefficiency arising from monopoly or monospony, and appreciate the shortcomings of price and rate-of-return regulation.
2. Distinguish a natural monopoly from a potentially competitive market.

3. Analyze how government regulation can resolve the economic inefficiency arising from asymmetric information.
4. Analyze how government regulation can resolve the economic inefficiency arising from externalities, and appreciate the differences between user fees and standards.
5. Appreciate the legal framework for resolution of the economic inefficiency in the provision of public goods.

Detailed Notes

1. Economic inefficiency and government regulation.

(a) Situations where marginal benefit diverges from marginal cost:
   i. Market power;
   ii. Asymmetric information;
   iii. Externalities and public goods.

(b) What government can regulate:
   i. Business structure;
   ii. Conduct;
   iii. Information.

2. Natural monopoly.

(a) Natural monopoly is a market where the average cost is minimized with a single supplier, e.g., distribution of electricity and water. A market is a natural monopoly when economies of scale or scope are large relative to market demand.
   i. If a market is a natural monopoly, the government should prohibit competition and award an exclusive franchise to a single supplier.
   ii. The monopoly might exploit its exclusive right to raise its price at the expense of its customers.

(b) Government ownership.
   i. A government-owned enterprise tends to be relatively inefficient.
      (1) More prone to be coopted by employees, resulting in high wages and over staffing, and inflating the costs of production.
      (2) Depends on the government for investment funds.
   ii. Privatization: Privatization is the transfer of ownership from the government to the private sector. A private enterprise may have an exclusive franchise and hence be a monopoly.

(c) Price regulation – the regulated price is fixed.
   i. Marginal cost pricing is the policy in which the price is set equal to marginal cost and the provider is required to supply the quantity demanded.
      (1) Production at economic efficient level: marginal benefit equals marginal cost.

(2) Government subsidy may be required to ensure that the business breaks even.

ii. Average cost pricing is the policy in which the price is set equal to average cost and the provider is required to supply the quantity demanded.

(1) With economies of scale:

a. Average cost curve is higher than marginal cost curve.

b. Lower level of provision than marginal cost pricing.

c. Provision is at economically inefficient level: marginal benefit equals average cost (franchise holder's price), not marginal cost.

iii. A provider subject to price regulation may exaggerate its reported costs to attempt to set a higher price.

(d) Rate of return regulation – franchise holder can set prices freely, provided it does not exceed the maximum allowed rate of return (profit) on the value of the rate base.

i. The rate base is the assets to which the rate of return regulation applies.

ii. The franchise holder's prices are required to be reduced if its rate of return exceeds the specified maximum.

iii. Three difficulties.

(1) Disputes over appropriate rate of return – there may be few comparable investments to provide benchmark rate of return.

(2) Disputes over assets constituting the rate base required to provide the service.

(3) A provider subject to rate of return regulation may invest in rate base beyond the economically efficient level, and so obtain higher profit.

3. Potentially competitive market.

(a) With changes in technology or market demand, a market may shift from being a natural monopoly to potentially competitive market, or vice versa.

i. A potentially competitive market is one where economies of scale or scope are small relative to market demand.

(1) These markets should be open to competition.

(2) Government protection such as exclusive franchises or restrictions against imports are anti-competitive.

ii. If perfect competition prevails over a potentially competitive market, the invisible hand ensures economic efficiency.

iii. Regulated industries are subject to laws specific to the industry, and may also be subject to general competition law.

(b) Structural regulation. A natural monopoly may have upstream or downstream markets that are potentially competitive.

i. Monopoly franchise holder may also participate in the potentially competitive market (e.g., holder of monopoly franchise over distribution of water vertically integrates upstream into the production of water).

ii. Structural regulation is a way to separate a natural monopoly from upstream or downstream markets that are potentially competitive, e.g., compulsory divestment of one of the businesses.

4. Asymmetric Information.

(a) Information asymmetry may be resolved through government regulations.

(b) Disclosure. The better-informed party is required by the government to disclose its information truthfully. Note: Information should be objectively verifiable.

(c) Regulation of conduct. The better informed party is regulated to limit the extent to which it can exploit its informational advantage, e.g., requirements for agreements to be in writing, waiting periods, recommending second opinions be obtained.

(d) Structural regulations (on the better informed party). Separation of different businesses, e.g.,

- i. Separation of audit services from consulting;
- ii. Separation of medical advice and treatment from sale of pharmaceuticals;
- iii. Separate representation of buyer and seller in real estate transactions.

(e) Self-regulation is the regulation of industry members by an industry organization.

- i. The trade organization may specify rules of conduct, regulations of business structures.
- ii. However, exclusive right to license practitioners may be a cover to limit competition.

5. Externalities.

(a) Private action may fail to resolve widespread externalities involving large numbers of parties.

- i. The economically efficient level of an externality balances the social marginal benefit with social marginal cost (sum of marginal costs to individual victims).
- ii. The efficient degree of an externality varies with location and time.

(b) User fees.

- i. These allow all sources to emit pollutants as much as they like provided that they pay a user fee.
  - (1) The user fee is set for all sources of emissions at the social marginal cost of emissions.
  - (2) It balances social marginal benefit of emissions with social marginal cost, and achieves the economically efficient level of emissions.

(c) Standards.

- i. Set the standard at the economically efficient level of emissions.
- ii. If the cost of monitoring is low, the standard may be implemented through a licensing scheme: Sell fixed number of user licenses through public auction to all sources. At equilibrium price, the price of each license

equals the social marginal cost of emissions, same as a user fee determined by a competitive market.

(1) The demand of each source of pollution for licenses will be the same as its marginal benefit from emissions.

(2) The market demand equals the horizontal sum of the individual demand curves; the market demand curve is identical to the social marginal benefit curve.

(3) Each source's emissions and the total emissions will be economically efficient.

iii. If the cost of monitoring is high for certain sources, it may be more cost-efficient to directly specify the standard to each user.

(d) Regional and temporal differences.

i. If the benefits and costs of an externality are confined to a region, it is economically efficient to allow each region to determine its own degree of the externality.

ii. National or international standards are necessary for externalities that cross boundaries.

iii. If the marginal benefit and the marginal cost of an externality vary over time, the efficient degree of the externality will also vary with time.

(e) Accidents.

i. The economically efficient level of care balances the social marginal benefit of care (in terms of reduced harm from accidents) with the marginal cost of care to the driver.

ii. The law of torts governs interaction between parties that have no contractual relationship.

(1) Specifies the liability of the parties to an accident (set of conditions under which one party must pay damages to another) and the damages.

(2) Each potential injurer will balance the private marginal benefit of care (in terms of the reduced expected liability for damages) against the marginal cost.

(3) Guides potential injurers to choose the economically efficient level of care.

6. Public goods.

(a) A public good provides nonrival consumption or use. It may be provided: on a commercial basis (privately), by charity, or the government.

i. Economic efficient level of provision: marginal benefit equals marginal cost (zero).

(b) Legal framework.

i. A public good can be provided commercially only if it is excludable. Excludability depends on legal framework and technology.

ii. During the life of a patent or copyright, the owner has an exclusive right. The owner will set a price higher than the marginal cost of usage.

The user's marginal benefit equals the price. So, usage is less than efficient.

iii. Upon expiration of the patent or copyright, usage extends to the point where marginal benefit equals zero, which is economically efficient.

iv. Intellectual property must balance the trade-off

(1) Stronger property right – greater financial incentive to the inventor/creator;

(2) Weaker property right – more use of the good.

(c) Public provision.

i. This is one way to provide public goods that are not excludable or are difficult to exclude.

ii. If no price is charged, the good will be used up to the quantity where marginal benefit equals zero, which is economically efficient.

(d) Congestible facilities (e.g., tunnels, roads, subways).

i. User fees for congestible facilities (e.g., tolls) should be set equal to the marginal cost of use, where the cost includes the negative externalities imposed on other users.

(1) Hence user fees should vary with demand for the facility: as marginal cost (including externalities) varies during the day, so should the fees.

(e) Social versus private benefits.

i. Intellectual property strategy and patents in particular play a strong role in R&D decisions.

ii. Much of the rationale for patents hinges on the tradeoff between the inefficiency of granting monopoly power to the inventor and providing adequate incentives for invention.

iii. There are two important countervailing factors to the finding that investment in R&D will be less than socially optimal.

(1) First, most invention and innovation is simultaneously pursued by a number of organizations. Thus, the effect of much R&D is to accelerate invention and innovation, but not to determine whether or not it occurs.

(2) Second, many patented products are substitutes for products that are currently provided at a price that exceeds marginal cost (due to patents on the currently available substitute products).

Answers to Progress Checks

15A. See figure 15A on page 458 of the textbook.

15B. One operator should be given a monopoly franchise for distribution of gas. It should be either not allowed to produce natural gas or required to separate its distribution and production businesses.

15C. See figure 15C on page 459 of the textbook. With a $25 per ton user fee, sources of emissions will emit 1.3 million tons a year. Social benefit would be area 0agn, under the marginal benefit curve up to 1.3 million tons a year. Social cost would be area 0dfn, under the marginal cost curve up to 1.3 million tons a year. There would be a net social gain of area aed less area efg. With a $45 per ton user fee, there would be a net social gain of area abcd. Neither the $25 nor the $45 fee is optimal. Which is preferable depends on the balance between area bec and area efg.

15D. The new level of care would exceed the economically efficient level.

15E. Reduce.

15F. Assuming that demand varies over the day, the marginal cost of usage will also vary. Economically efficient usage requires the price to vary with the marginal cost.

Answers to Review Questions

1. [Omitted].

2. Price regulation targets the provider's cost and gives it an incentive to exaggerate its reported costs. Rate of return regulation targets the provider's rate base and gives it an incentive to invest beyond the economically efficient level.

3. Price regulation targets the provider's cost and gives it an incentive to exaggerate its reported costs. If prices are permitted to change over time, a mechanism needs to be established which accounts for expected technological advances, expected cost increases, and exogenous impacts on the regulated firm's profitability.

4. Rate of return regulated companies have little incentive to minimize costs and have exaggerated incentives to increase their rate base. There are also significant administrative costs with implementing such regulation (determining the rate base, the rate of return, and monitoring costs).

5. Privatization means transferring ownership from the public to the private sector. Allowing competition means removing an exclusive right.

6. [Omitted].

7. (a) A movie producer that owns a theater is vertically integrated into the exhibition business. (b) The law that prohibited movie producers from owning theaters is a structural regulation to separate the movie production and exhibition businesses.

8. False.

9. Regulation of conduct and structure may prevent the party with superior information from exploiting that advantage, and so resolve the information asymmetry.

10. (a) The regulator could charge a fee for noise generated by the construction equipment. (b) The regulator could set a standard and make it illegal for construction equipment to generate noise exceeding the standard.

11. False.

12. They give the owner the legal power to exclude others from usage.

13. (a) Not an externality because all the parties belong to the market for production workers. (b) This is an externality.

14. No.

15. Private good provides rival consumption/usage; public good provides nonrival consumption/usage; congestible facility provides usage that is rival when usage reaches capacity.

Sample Answer to Discussion Question

1. In July 2000, the San Diego Water Authority charged its 23 member agencies a uniform price of $439 per acre-foot of water. (An acre-foot is the volume of water that would cover one acre to a depth of one foot, or about 326,000 gallons.) Suppose that the Water Authority practices marginal-cost pricing and its marginal cost of water is increasing and begins at $0.
   (a) Illustrate the current price and quantity on an appropriate diagram.
   (b) The Water Authority negotiated with the Imperial Irrigation District to buy 200,000 acre-feet of Colorado River water at $245 per acre-foot. Show how this purchase would affect the Authority's marginal cost of water.
   (c) Assume that the Water Authority continues to practice marginal cost pricing. On your diagram, show the increase in buyer and seller surplus that San Diego as a whole will achieve from the acquisition of the 200,000 acre-feet.

Answer:

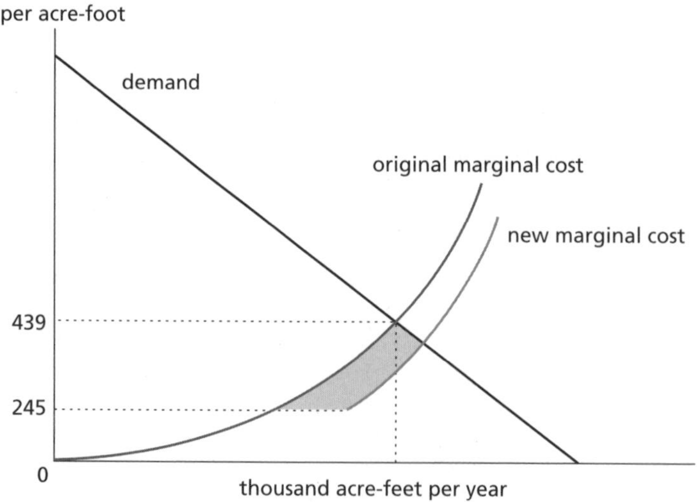

(a) The current price and quantity are at the intersection of the demand and (original) marginal cost curves.
(b) The new marginal cost curve follows the original curve up to the $245 level, then runs flat for 200,000 acre-feet, then continues upward like the original marginal cost curve.
(c) Under marginal cost pricing, the new price will be at the intersection of the demand and new marginal cost curves. The increase in buyer and seller surplus is the shaded area.